Business for the Right-Brained

The Three Jaguars Present:

Business for the Right-Brained

M.C.A. Hogarth

mcahogarth.org

Business for the Right-Brained
Three Jaguars Books

First edition, copyright 2018 by M.C.A. Hogarth

M. Hogarth
PMB 109
4522 West Village Dr.
Tampa, FL 33624

ISBN-13: 978-1985663039
ISBN-10: 1985663031

Cover and interior art by M.C.A. Hogarth

Designed and typeset by Catspaw DTP Services
http://www.catspawdtp.com/

This one's for May. Thank you for lending me your Inner Financial Advisor. ♥

Table of Contents

Foreword

THERE'S AN OLD SILICON VALLEY joke that says that many startup businesses have a plan that looks like something out of South Park:

Step 1: Make the thing.
Step 2: ?????
Step 3: Profit.

In recent years, technology and culture have allowed artists to create their own startup businesses. On the face of it, it seems easy: you're the only person creating your art, so no need for employees or even a good deal of funding. You write books, create music, record videos, draw pictures, and there are people who like them and could probably be persuaded to buy them. Plus, the news is full of YouTube celebrities and self-published authors and indie musicians worth millions.

And yet, many artists seeking to monetize their art fall into trap of skipping the aforementioned step 2. Today's landscape presents a number of opportunities for an enterprising artist, yes, but just as many pitfalls, and few of those are obvious. Why doesn't your work sell as well as your friend's, or a tenth as well as that slightly more famous person's? What do you do when everyone's moving to a new pricing scheme? What happens when the platform where you were selling your work changes their rules, or just up and vanishes? What can you do to make sure you don't burn out on your art?

Of all the people I can think of to help answer these questions, M.C.A. Hogarth tops the list. She's worked for years as an artist and writer and has had work professionally published as well as doing all the publishing herself. For years she balanced a day job and family against the career of an author, and she's also worked on behalf of other small press and self-published authors within the Science Fiction and Fantasy Writers of America (SFWA).

Beyond just the hands-on experience, though, Maggie has impressed me time and again with the observation and analysis she puts into her business. Whenever I talk shop with her, she's always ready with facts about whatever we're discussing, or else she formulates a plan to find out what she doesn't know.

Then we can switch gears from talking about the business of writing to talking about the work, and she goes from talking about her books as the products she sells to being one hundred percent Author, with stories she's excited to write and difficult patches and anxiety over what the beta readers are going to say. Not many authors can do that.

So I was delighted to find out that all of that jaguar wisdom

Business for the Right-Brained

is being recorded in a handy volume, and I'm honored to introduce you to it. Herein you'll find many secrets to successfully navigating your own "step 2," not tied to current platforms but in the more useful form of strategies to navigate a changing world. When I started publishing e-books in 2009, the landscape was vastly different than it is today, and the same is true for artists of any type. Nobody knows for sure where the opportunities for tomorrow's self-employed artist will be, but having this book will help you be prepared to take advantage of them, wherever they appear.

—Kyell Gold
Mountain View, CA

Introduction: Priorities, or Knowing What You Really Want

EVERY TIME I RUN A BUSINESS seminar or write a business column, I start with the assumption that everyone attending or reading wants to have a career in the arts field; that in basic, they're there to learn how to treat their art like a business and make money off it. And every time I run a business seminar or write a business column, I forget that before you pursue a career, you have to decide you want one.

I WANT THIS! I'M TOTALLY READY FOR IT! I THINK! MAYBE... UM...

This decision is not an easy one.

Our society treats money as a metric for assessing worth. This works well enough that we try to apply it to everything, even things it's not at all suited for measuring. Sometimes, it's obvious that money makes a poor measuring stick: we instinctively understand that love can't be translated into money, nor can community. But there are gray areas where ideas mingle with products and create confusion, and art is one of them. Art can be turned into products or experiences that can earn money, so people immediately glom onto money as a measurement of its value.

That this sometimes works muddies the waters further.

A lot of artists go into art careers because they have absorbed the cultural message that unless they're earning money, their work is worthless. Diving into art-as-a-business is a way of validating their desire to make art, and to protect that desire from people who tell them they're wasting their time ("You spend too much time doodling! Get a real job!"). But this decision, which usually happens at the subconscious level, often leads to heartbreak; partially because money is a poor indicator of the worth of a work of art, and partially because without externalizing our reasons for how we prefer to engage with our work, we fail to meet our own needs.

The majority of artists didn't start making art because they wanted money. Most of us got into our fields because we love what we do. Before we decide to productize our work, we need to decide what we want out of our relationship with art.

Here are some common things people want out of their work:

- **A Dialogue With Yourself:** Many of us use our work to work out our feelings, process our experiences, or make sense of our lives. Sometimes things aren't real until we write them

Business for the Right-Brained

down, or dance them out; we don't expunge our grief or understand our reactions to things without externalizing them in a form we can manipulate.

- **Engagement with an Audience:** Many of us like the interaction sharing our work inspires. It makes us feel closer to other people, like we have things in common; it gives us things to talk about. It makes us feel less alone.

- **Fame within a Community:** Many of us enjoy being known for what we do. We get a buzz when people say they recognize our work, or that we're esteemed enough to be invited to special projects, speaking engagements, or organizations. It's satisfying to be considered a subject matter expert in something we consider important to our lives.

- **The Challenge of Perfecting a Craft:** Many of us love the feeling of getting better at something we do all the time. The charge of learning new techniques, feeling we've broken free of another plateau, or can reach the heights that we aspired to as newer artists, is highly motivating.

- **The Pleasure of Making Things:** Many of us love the pleasure of making something out of nothing: whether it's a physical object that didn't exist before we put our hands on a material, or an idea that we developed into something easier to share. Sometimes it's a meditative exercise, and we derive peace from it; sometimes it's an exultation, and we get a high from it. Sometimes it's hard, but when we finish the satisfaction of being able to enjoy that final form is deeply enriching.

- **A Way of Retreating From (or Relaxing Into) the World:** Many of us need an escape, and making art is a way of getting ourselves some needed distance from a world that is cacophonous, too fast, too intense, or too in our faces . . . and some of us need a way to slide into the world, and art leads us there.

- **Money:** Finally, many of us like the feeling that we have a skill that translates into money. Or we just like buying groceries.

Realize that the moment the last reason becomes your most important reason, you will have to compromise on all the others. Monetizing your work comes with many, many cons. Here are only a few of the situations or problems that crop up when you decide to start selling your work:

- **You can no longer choose not to work.** If you don't do the work, you don't make money. There's no more 'I'd rather read a book or talk online with friends.' In fact, you'll find it hard to justify taking any time off, even for necessary things, like health, family, leisure.

- **You can no longer work at your own pace.** Slow artists rarely produce enough work to make enough money to stay afloat.

- **You can no longer choose what to work on.** Those commissions you took and don't really feel? Will have to be done anyway. The series that's selling will often be the one you wish you could close the door on. The symphony you want to write won't work well sampled into 2 minute bites for youtubers to buy for their videos.

- **You now have an (arbitrary) metric to use to compare yourself to your peers.** Before, you had no idea if you were "better" than other people. Now you'll be able to say things like "that person whose work is less skilled than mine is making three times as much as me." Or worse, you'll guess this is true, but not be sure because no one divulges their income.

- **You will become one of those people who doesn't divulge their income**—if it's too little, out of shame and embarrassment; if it's too much, out of fear of other people's envy and anger; if it seems enough, out of worry that it will inspire other people to share their incomes with you, and illuminate that you're wrong about doing pretty well.

- **Your peers will begin thinking of you as competition.** While this isn't universally true, there is a reason why artists talk with such admiration about peers who build other artists up, rather than rip them down.

- **People will judge you more harshly based on your prices.** When people buy things, they demand a lot more out of them. The moment you acquire customers rather than an audience, you will be obliged to give them value for their dollar . . . and you and your customers may disagree on whether you've done enough.

- **People will treat you as interchangeable with other similar artists.** You will discover that many people shop based on price, and that you can be passed over in favor of someone cheaper without any heartache on their parts.

- **You will no longer be able to "be yourself" without consequences.** The things you say, your political and religious beliefs, and your lifestyle will suddenly become pertinent to buyers, and they will make decisions based on those things. If you're lucky, for you. But you won't always—or even often—be lucky, which means you'll have to decide how much of your "real" self you want to keep hidden.

- **You will have to keep track of every dollar you earn and spend.** Tracking receipts never sounds too bad; tedious maybe, but not bad. But you will have to squirrel out all the hidden costs as well. Your con table is never "the table cost + the airfare + the hotel bill." It's also "how much food I ate, the Paypal/Square fees that took a percentage of every in-person sale, the in-state taxes, the fact that the time I spent there was time not spent doing new work," etc, etc.

- **You will have to analyze your work, which might lead you to unpleasant discoveries.** You might assume that something you thought would sell really well, and that seems to be selling really well, is actually a dud. Or the work you spent the longest on is the work that sells least well. (Or conversely, the quick commissions you thought were shoring up your income are, in fact, losing you money.) This extends into ways of working too: those conventions you think are so much fun might actually be so bad for your profitability that you might have to give them up.

- **You will no longer think of your work as a fun refuge;** every time you do it, you will unavoidably begin thinking about whether it can earn you anything. You will also find yourself analyzing everyone else's work too; many people say they lose the ability to enjoy art as an audience once they've started selling it.

- **Your work may not ever earn you enough money, and you will find yourself resenting it for not being enough.** "It means so much to me; why doesn't it matter to other people?" "Why do I work so hard, and yet never make enough?" "Why do I have this talent if it can't even buy me a cheap loaf of bread?" "Why don't people understand that art doesn't come from nowhere?" "Why don't they care enough about me to help me succeed?" The list of ways you can get angry about not succeeding are endless . . . and worst of all:

- **Your goalposts will move.** When you first start out, your goals will be modest: "Make $10 this month." But once you hit those goals, you won't be satisfied. They'll become "Make $100 a month," and then "$1000 a month." (Or 600 reviews, or 500 downloads, or 10,000 watchers, or 10 awards). For most people, there's never a good enough.

These are just some of the ways going into business as an artist will affect your relationship with art. Consider that last carefully and compare it against the ways art feeds your soul. If what you need from your art doesn't align with what you have to do to make money at it, you should seriously consider whether you want to pursue art as a business venture.

In no universe should you think of your decision *not* to pursue art as a business venture a failure. (In fact, in some circles, you're a failure if you *do* pursue it as a business venture!) Money does not define your worth as an artist. It exists to put food on your table—that's all. But once you get involved with it, the temptation to continually assess yourself by the one metric—money—will almost invariably overwhelm your ability to hold on to the more ephemeral or abstract reasons you love doing the work, and you will find it very hard not to find your world narrowing to 'how much money has this earned for me today.'

If this is a burden you don't want, don't go there. It's *totally okay* not to go there. Many amazing works of art have been produced by people who saved their art for after they were done with their money-making activities, and they were not less beautiful, worthy, or compelling because they were done in someone's 'spare time.'

So! Before you read any of these business columns, sit down and make a list of reasons why you make art, and what you get out of sharing it. Be honest! There are no wrong answers. Decide whether you can get what you need from your work without productizing it, or if in fact productizing it might poison the well for you altogether. Once you get your list, prioritize the results. Is it more important for you to explore your inner issues, or to share your work with an audience? Do you like the feeling of being known in a community more than you like existing as a small fish in a big pond, the way most of us must if we're chasing remuneration?

Until you do this step, you will flounder your way through the business stuff, or worse, you will be miserable and not know why.

Many an artist has decided they'd rather make soy lattes than lose their sense of joy in their work, or feel beholden to deadlines or projects they don't care about. You will not be a lesser artist for joining their ranks: you will be a *happier* one, and happier artists create better work, and often more work, and take more pleasure from it. Plus, it frees you to occasionally sell your work without the pressure of having to do it all the time. Remember: life is rarely a series of black and white choices. Deciding to sell your work as a hobbyist is as valid a choice as not selling it at all, or embarking on art as a career professional.

Turning your art into a career involves a great deal of back-breaking labor, frustration, and a persistent sense that you can't control your own success (because you can't; 100% of this business is luck, and the other 100% is working like a mule, and the two have no connection). The rewards can be worthwhile, but you can't earn them without compromises.

It may be that you're not sure whether you want to go the business route or not, and if so, I hope this book will illuminate enough of what's entailed to allow you to make an educated decision. (Or it may be that you feel you have no choice, and that you need to make money somehow, at which point I hope this book helps you make the best of a bad situation.) But knowing what you need is paramount to keeping your soul intact. So figure that out now, and then, turn the page.

Many Roles

OUR FIRST STEP IN EMBARKING on any business endeavor as an artist is to realize that there's more than one role involved in making a business work. The moment you hand over something in return for money, you're no longer just the Artist . . . now your concerns have expanded to include how to handle money, how to get your art into people's hands, and how to arrange things so both those things happen more often.

By my way of thinking, there are three basic roles: Business Manager, Marketer, and Artist. Artist can be taken to mean any artistic endeavor: writing, craft-making, singing . . . whatever you're trying to make money on. Veterans of larger companies will note that I've folded Sales into Marketing, which is a personal bias. Don't worry, Marketer's pretty energetic, she can handle it.

Without further ado, then, the Three Jaguars!

Business Manager

Primary Workmode: *Practical and Administrative*

Your Business Manager self needs to channel an inner Virgo (if you have one): meticulous, data-focused and completist. This is the self that makes lists and does chores and says, "Uh, no" to things like "Can I buy a crazy-expensive thing that we can't afford."

Since I don't have an inner Virgo, I think of the Business Manager as my inner Parent; they both say 'no' a lot.

Duties

- **Accounting:** The primary duty of the Business Manager is accounting: tracking expenses and revenue and calculating profit. That means every time money comes in, you write it down, and every time money goes out, you write it down . . . and then you subtract the one from the other to see how you're doing. The Business Manager is also in charge of maintaining lists of customers, tracking layaways or recurring purchases/income and preparing taxes.

I LIKE DATA ENTRY. AND COFFEE. ALSO, SPREADSHEETS.

- **Personnel Management:** Your Business Manager self is also charged with time-tracking: this means that you need to know how long *everything you do* takes, whether it's marketing, creative work or your business management tasks. That really does mean *everything*. Runs to the post office, inputting income, drawing a new picture, researching a new art supply, social-networking, composing blog posts; all of that is a cost of doing business, and you need to record it. The Marketer will need this data to help advise the Business Manager which tasks are more profitable than others.

- **Asset Management:** The Business Manager also tracks (and depreciates) all your assets, manages inventory and replaces or re-orders necessary parts. This is the part of you that shows up to sort and label all your existing work, figures out if you need to buy a new computer or brushes and purchases another year of your post office box when the rent comes due.

- **Process Management:** All businesses have processes . . . and the Business Manager should always be on the look-out for ways to streamline yours. If you spend less time on processes, you have more time to do everything else. Things like deciding to run all your business errands on the same day so that you aren't constantly interrupting your studio time to hit the post office fall under process-management.

- **Administrative:** This is the Self that goes out and mails out things, deposits checks, packages products for mailing, buys pens and papers and coffee.

Facing: *Vendor and Financial Institutions*
The Business Manager is the one buying things (with a jaundiced eye and a tight fist) and interacting with banks and financial institutions.

Outsourcing Potential: *Medium.*
You can get people do so some of the work of the Business Manager; it's not too hard to get someone to label things and mail them for you. You can pay for someone to prepare your taxes. This can be moderately expensive, depending on where you are or whether you have access to artist organizations. The cons? A lot of Business Management requires close interaction with you on a day-to-day basis, or exchange of personal information. Getting other people to help you streamline your processes can be hit-or-miss if they don't know your daily routine or your personal situation.

Business for the Right-Brained

Business Manager Worksheet

It's time to get to know your inner Business Manager! As we just discussed, Business Manager does the accounting, personnel and asset management, process management, and administrative work. Here are some basic questions to get you started on those areas.

1. Are you tracking your incoming money and outgoing money? Are you comfortable with how you're doing this? (Are you doing it manually, on paper? On a spreadsheet? With specialized software?)

2. Do you have an idea of what your assets are? These are all your tools, equipment, property (including your home office or studio). Your computer, your paint, your printers, your software, your recording studio, your bins of gemstones . . . all these things are assets! Maybe you should make a list . . . Business Manager loves lists!

3. Do you know any of your customers' names? Do you work with any freelancers—editors, artists, distributors, etc? Do you maintain a database of useful business contacts?

4. Do you know about how long it takes you to do your art? (A discrete piece: one novel, one cosplay costume, one

song, etc). Do you know how long it takes for you to sell it (by posting it online, by taking it to a shop, by mailing it to a commissioner, etc)? How could you track that information so that you'd stay on top of the data gathering?

5. Are the basic steps by which you make and sell your work the same every time you do it, or do they change? Do you feel like your processes are so predictable that you could document them as a flow chart?

Don't worry if you don't have answers to these questions yet! These are intended to help you sense the job responsibilities of your inner Business Manager. Maybe you already do some of this . . . maybe you do none of it! But just considering the questions will help you begin to answer them.

Marketer

Primary Workmode: *Creative and Social*

Your Marketer self is the one that spends most of her time thinking about, interacting with or guessing at what other people want. This can be a surprisingly creative process. The first questions she holds in her mind are: "How would I like to be treated as a customer? What kinds of things would I love to buy?" (followed closely by "How do other people seem to like to be treated? What kinds of things do they seem to like to buy?") . . . which means you spend a lot of time delighting yourself by figuring out what makes you happy and trying to do that for other people.

Duties

- **Trend Analysis:** Your inner Marketer is in charge of taking sales, revenue and expense data and using it to figure out which of your tasks are the most profitable. For instance, the Marketer might notice that selling prints at a show takes roughly 20 hours and makes $800 before expenses and $600 afterwards . . . while selling a single original might take 8 hours, make $500 before expenses and $450 after; this would lead your Marketer to tell Business Manager and Artist at their next meeting: "Hey, stop going to shows and produce more originals."

> I LIKE PEOPLE! AND CHARTS. AND SHINY THINGS!

- **Customer Care:** The Marketer is also in charge of dealing with customers. She's the one who figures out how to attract them, the one who closes the sale (and decides how to manage the sale process to make the customer feel special) and the one who keeps in touch with them afterwards to see if they're interested in new products. The Marketer's also the one who deals with problems: yours (oops, I was late delivering something I promised: here's my apology and a coupon or free cool thing) or theirs (ack, the post office broke your handmade bowl, let's discuss what we can do about that).

- **Product Management:** Your Marketer is the one who develops new products and maintains existing ones. There's more than one way to sell an artist's labor; the art you make is not a product until the Marketer figures out how to sell it. You might choose to license it, sell commissioned work, package it as a book, sell it as prints, collaborate with someone else to create a different item . . . the possibilities are as endless as your imagination.

- **Research and Advertising:** When you sit down to update blogs, do social networking, respond to customer queries, enter contests, send work to juried shows, design fliers or contact the local paper to offer an interview, it's your Marketer who's doing the work of advertising. She's also the one charged with research to see what your peers are up to: how are they marketing themselves? What products are they offering, and can they be adapted to your work-style? What's hot now?

Facing: *Customer*
The Marketer is the one dealing with patrons, audience, customers. You should always have your best face forward for them!

Outsourcing Potential: *Medium-to-High.*
Of all the roles you've got, Marketing and Advertising can respond the best to outsourcing (in my experience). You can hire people to run and create your website. You can buy books or read blogs that basically tell you what kind of products to sell or how to sell them. You can hire advertising firms, if you're

Business for the Right-Brained

so minded. The problem? It's very expensive. It also means your marketing is less customized to your product and work-style, which can become a problem.

Marketer Worksheet

The bubbly, social personality of your inner Marketer might be your least familiar interior personality! Nevertheless, they're hiding in there somewhere. Here are some questions that might help you get to know your Marketer.

1. How much research do you do on other artists' business practices? Do you keep up on what your peers are doing and how they're selling their work?

2. How often do you talk about your work on an outlet that could be construed as advertisement, like a blog, or Facebook, twitter, tumblr, etc?

3. How often do you interact with your audience? Do you know any of them by name? Do you have any repeat customers that you know of? Superfans?

4. What do you do when something goes wrong with something you sell? How do you handle the resulting complaints?

5. How do you decide it's time to try selling something new? What kind of thought process do you use to develop new things you could sell people, or new ways to reach them?

6. Do you go out into the world to interact with your audience? If so, where? What's your attitude about those things? Do you enjoy it or dread it? Do you put conscious thought into how you present yourself when you are going somewhere as your artist-self?

Again, don't be worried if you don't have good answers for these questions yet. Getting to know your Inner Marketer is a process, like everything else involved in setting up a business. If you have any thoughts in response to the list, though . . . jot them down!

Artist

Primary Workmode: *Creative and Internal*
Nose to the grindstone in your studio! Here's the raison d'etre for the whole business.

Duties
- **Creation:** Your number one job as an artist is to make stuff. That's probably the reason we all signed up for this, after

I LIKE DRAWING. <3

all. But this is ironclad: you really have to make things. You can't sit in a studio and think about making things. You can't say you're going to make things and never get around to it. You can't make things irregularly. If you're doing this as full-time work, you should be sitting in a chair doing it for most of the day.

- **Research:** Your other job as an artist is research. Not just what other artists are doing, though that can be helpful. You should be researching your craft (has some new technology come out that's made things easier or better? Is there a new technique you can learn somewhere?). You should be experimenting, both with the art itself and with the processes you use to create it. Your goal should be to develop as an artist, because there's no holding steady. You're either improving or stagnating. Entropy is law in this universe, and you are no less subject to it than anything else.

- **Practice:** Related to research is practice: you should be improving your skills. This relates not just to technique, but how quickly you can turn your work around. Practice is also the only thing that will allow you to learn to estimate your time-per-project, an essential skill: this will allow you to set realistic deadlines and feed data to the Marketer about how much time it takes for you to create something.

Facing: *Internal*
Your creative self should be quieter than your other selves when interacting with people; by nature most people's inner Artists are passionate and that passion can often clash badly

with your need to be an empathic salesperson. A lot of artists also find that talking about their work gets in the way of them doing it: they lose their interest after discussing it, or they find themselves discussing it as a way to procrastinate.

Outsourcing Potential: *Low*
Only you can do the work!

Artist Checklist
Do we really need an artist checklist? Don't we already know our inner Artist pretty well?? Maybe you'll be surprised! Check out these questions, see if they shake anything loose:

- Do you research new materials? New methods? How often do you try new media or new ideas?

- How many of your peers do you follow? Are they doing anything interesting or inspiring?

- What kind of practice do you do to improve? Do you have any technical goals for yourself? Milestones you'd like to hit as an artist (for visual artists, for instance, "I'd like to be able to draw backgrounds better.")

- How fast can you produce work? Do you ever

practice specifically to become faster at what you do? Do you think you could improve your speed . . . if not by improving the actual physical work, but by tightening up your processes? (If, for instance, it takes two hours to make a piece of jewelry but your supplies are scattered all over the room so that you're constantly standing up to get things, is there a way to rearrange your studio so that all your supplies are at arms' length?)

- Do you become inspired when you talk about what you're doing? Or does it drain your interest? Are you always that way, or does it depend?

Many people find their inner artists don't really like talking about process that much, which is great if you're doing art as a hobby. Unfortunately, consistently producing work for money requires a level of scrutiny that hobby Artists can escape. Reassure your inner Artist (with prize of choice) and meditate on these questions, if you don't know their answers yet.

Now that we've met the three Jaguars we're ready to move on!

Products

So let's talk about products. Yes, products . . . you have them! Or you will. Let's start with . . .

Definitions

First and most importantly: what comes off the Artist's desk is not a product. A new painting is not a product. A new story is not a product. These things are turned into products by the Marketer, who targets an audience, packages it to appeal to them and then finds ways to sell it to them.

So, the new painting is not a product. But the prints that the Marketer sells to people with budgets for fine art reproductions are. The original, which the Marketer targets at people who are looking to become fine art collectors is. The downloadable wallpaper that the Marketer posts for free "but tip if you feel inclined!" is. A short story is not a product, but the story sold to a magazine to reach its audience is. The short story repackaged as a serial for blog readers is. The same short story offered as an incentive, included in an omnibus as new material, is.

The Artist produces stuff. But that stuff is not a product until the Marketer decides how best to sell something based on it. Your Artist should never be thinking about how to sell her stuff *because she's bad at it.* Not only that, but if she starts fretting about how to sell something before she's done it, one of two things will usually happen: 1. She'll stop up completely and be incapable of working, because she doesn't actually want to do things she thinks are "sellable;' or 2. She'll start producing drek she doesn't really believe in and then pitch a fit when nobody wants it, because nobody wants to buy art from someone who's faking it.

MERMAIDS ARE IN BUT I HATE DRAWING MERMAIDS WILL ANYONE BUY MY STUPID MERMAIDS AAAHHHH

Don't let your inner Marketer tell your Artist what to do, either: her job is not to force the Artist to produce something to meet

Business for the Right-Brained

existing demand, but to create demand for the Artist. If you're doing what everyone else is doing, you are replaceable. If you make it clear to people why what you're doing is cool and special, then people will come to you for your kind of cool and special. They might choose to spend money elsewhere one day, but it won't be because they can get what you make anywhere, it will be because something else will have become more valuable to them.

Let's move on to the two major categories of products, then.

New Work

What is it? I define new work as art that neither the Artist nor the audience has seen: the Artist because she hasn't made it yet and the audience because it doesn't exist.

Why do it? I'll let the Three Jaguars answer:

In short, you need new art to keep your Artist happy: she needs to improve her craft and work on things that are exciting her, because chances are if it excites her it will excite her audience. Audiences like to see an artist creating new work because they like to feel invested in artists they like, and they don't want to dump energy into an artist they feel is winding down in their career.

New work gives your Marketer potential new products to package on a regular basis, which allows you to grow your audience through frequent (and predictable) updates/releases.

But wait! you say. The Artist isn't producing work predictably!

Of course she's not. But the Marketer isn't selling your art, she's selling the products she bases on your art. So staggered releases (original first, prints next, wallpapers a month later) give the Marketer something to sell at predictable intervals even if your Artist isn't producing regularly. We'll handle what to do if your Artist isn't producing regularly enough for even the most creative inner Marketer in our next section.

Meanwhile, the Business Manager is happy because new work = new opportunities to make money. You can't make money without something to sell. People are more likely to spring for new work because they haven't seen it before, and because new car smell is very exciting. We all like to feel like we're in on something at the ground floor. Plus, if we're an existing fan of an artist, we've already consumed their existing products . . . we want the next thing.

Examples

- **Art:** Putting a new painting for sale in a gallery.

- **Writing:** Releasing a new short story as a serial online.

- **Music:** Offering a new song for download.

- **Jewelry:** Stringing a new necklace and putting it up on Etsy.

Your Turn

It's time to brainstorm some products based on new work! Remember: your work is not a product. It has to be packaged for sale in a specific manner in order to become a product!

To start this process, first define your discipline (writing, dancing, art, etc).

Next, imagine finishing a new piece of art. What's your most common type of art to finish? A novel-length story? Choreography for a performance?

Now, imagine the ways that people consume your particular art. Writers might think of people reading from web archives on phones, or e-books on e-book readers, or magazines they've subscribed to, or newspapers. Dancers might think of performances done for local shows, choreography taught to new students in classes, youtube videos, or a reel for animators to use for real-time capture.

If you're stuck, try looking at what other successful artists in your field are doing to sell their work!

Jot down two or three ideas now!

Existing/Old Work

What is it? I define existing/old work as work that the Artist has seen, having already produced it; and that your audience may or may not have seen. Some of your older fans will have. The new fans won't. Some old fans will have seen it but won't remember it.

Why do it? The Three Jaguars return!

WELL, WE DID ALREADY SINK ALL THIS TIME AND MONEY INTO THIS... I HATE WASTE.

I BET WE COULD GET PEOPLE EXCITED ABOUT WORK THAT'S CURRENTLY EARNING US NO MONEY!

SIGH

I mentioned above that there will be times the Artist just isn't producing enough new work for the Marketer to sell at regular intervals . . . or for the Business Manager to pay the bills. In that case, it's time to haul out work the Artist has already completed and were never productized, in which case the Marketer gets to work figuring out how to package them for sale. Or, it's time to haul out work the Artist has already completed, the Marketer has already sold a few times . . . and recontextualize it, packaging it either to market to new fans or to interest old ones.

But wait! you say. Isn't that dishonest? Trying to get people to pay twice for something they've already bought once?

Maybe if that's what you're actually doing. But remember, your art is not the product. How the Marketer sells the art is your product. If you package the same piece of art in a way that adds new value, then you're not being dishonest, you're just offering a different option to people who've already seen it (and a new option to people who haven't). They can choose whether that new version is worth more money to them.

The Business Manager likes selling old work because half the work (the Artist creating it) has already been done, and she can make money on something for only half the effort (the Marketer re-packaging it). The Marketer likes it because she can fill in the gaps of her product line schedule, plus she can get new fans to pay for work that was new before they came on board. But inevitably revisiting old work bores the Artist, who longs to be working on something that has set her on fire. Even if the Artist is currently without inspiration, she's going to resent returning to stuff she feels she's grown out of or past . . . something we'll address in the last section. But first, some examples.

Examples

- **Art:** Cutting up old prints that haven't sold into bookmarks or pieces for sale to scrapbookers.

- **Writing:** Finding old stories published in several different magazines or anthologies and collecting them as a single themed volume.

- **Music:** Licensing an existing song to an author for use in their book trailer, or to someone for their Youtube video.

- **Jewelry:** Shortening necklaces that haven't sold into bracelets that can be sold for cheaper.

Your Turn

It's time to brainstorm some products based on existing work! Remember: your work is not a product. It has to be packaged for sale in a specific manner in order to become a product!

BLERG. GOTTA BE DONE, I GUESS.

Again, let's start this process by defining your discipline (writing, dancing, art, etc).

Next, think of a project you've finished (or mostly finished) and haven't tried to sell. Or have tried to sell and couldn't get anyone to pick up. Writers might think of trunked stories; artists of unsold originals.

Business for the Right-Brained

Now, imagine ways you could repurpose this work! Maybe your trunked novel could make a reappearance in a short story as a book that irritates the main character. Or you could find the interesting elements of it and transplant it to a new setting or genre to see what happens. Your old original might make a good phone wallpaper. Or, worse comes to worst, you could use it to write a blog post about unsuccessful pieces and how you'd do things differently!

Jot down two or three ideas now!

Incentivizing

Yes it is a word, and I'm not afraid to use it! As I mentioned above, your Artist longs to work on things that set her on fire . . . and if she isn't currently on fire for something, she kind of would rather not work at all. Not on new things that have lost that new-love luster, not on old things that she secretly hates because what she can do now is soooo much better.

At this point, you have to learn what secondary motivations compel your inner Artist. Most Artists have at least one primary motivating force, the mysterious drive responsible for them suddenly tearing off for the nearest tool when an idea strikes them. But when that fire dies, a lot of Artists can be nudged by other forces, none of which are as powerful but which can at least keep the momentum going.

Common motivators include:

- **Reward.** *"If I finish this, I'll go to the local sauna/get a fancy cup of coffee/play a game for an hour."* This is the most basic form of motivation, and while it works it's loaded with pitfalls: for one, you might get so used to working for rewards that if you don't have them you might feel unmoved. Also, rewarding yourself for every milestone can get very expensive, eliciting dagger-glares from Business Manager. If you want to reward yourself for your efforts, try to keep the rewards small, non-monetary and infrequent.

- **Audience Interaction.** *"If I finish this, people will say nice things about my art and that will make me feel warm*

and fuzzy!" This is a great artistic motivator! It's cheap and it works, often when nothing else will. The problem? It's almost completely outside your control. You can create a climate where people feel encouraged to comment, you can remove obstacles that prevent them from commenting, you can commit yourself to responding to them so that they'll feel more inclined to begin a conversation in the future . . . but if the art doesn't speak to people, if they're not feeling up to it, if they just didn't happen to be online or in the presence of your work that day . . . no comments. And if you get too used to comments or conversations with your audience, when you don't get them you tend to take it very personally, and what was a source of warm-fuzzies becomes not just a null, but an actual detriment: you might become too discouraged to work.

Nevertheless, I think we're all moved by that connection with our audience, so whether we can get it as often as we want or not, it's going to be an intrinsic part of our lives as artists.

- **Money. "If I finish this, I will make some money!"** In our current culture, we grow up soaked in the belief that money = validation, so if you're feeling really low you can use money as a reason to keep working. But as with Rewards, this can lead to real heartache down the line. People don't buy artwork for many reasons, not just because it doesn't speak to them. If you train yourself to believe that the only yardstick by which you measure an artist's worth is how much she makes, you are going to crash and burn emotionally the first time you hit a lull in receipts. You might be tempted to lower your prices to lift your sales and your flagging self-esteem, an act that will come back to bite you later.

If you do use money as a spur for your efforts, be sure you keep your inner Artist separate from your inner Business Manager. Imagine your Business Manager telling your Artist, "If you finish something, we might have a better chance of buying more chocolate," rather than having your inner Artist adopt the mantra, "If people pay me, it means I'm good."

- **Tools and Inspirations. *"Maybe if I get a new tool, go through some new books, I will feel more inspired!"*** For some people buying a new tool or thumbing through other people's work or reading a book or watching a show on something exotic and unknown to them is enough to get moving again. While this can lead to spending too much money ("oooh, a shiny new box of pastels!") or procrastination ("just one more show on ancient Egypt!"), it's still often healthier than some of the other methods. Just enlist the aid of your Business

Manager ("How much money am I allowed to spend?") and go for it.

- **The Chance to FIX THINGS.** *"Oh I hated how that old picture came out, maybe if I do it at my current skill level it won't suck so much . . ."* Most Artists are secret perfectionists who are never happy with the way something came out . . . or if they were then, looking back at it a year later makes them want to burn it with fire. A great motivator for that inner perfectionist is to give them the chance to fix old mistakes: revisit old pieces and try to improve them directly, or start from scratch and try to do better justice to the idea. This motivator costs nothing but time you would have spent anyway . . . and it also directly impacts skill level by encouraging your Artist to work at the limit of her skills.

You'll note a lot of these motivators are riddled with pitfalls and problems! But all of them are healthier than some of the other ways Artists motivate themselves: guilt ("I'm not working hard enough."), jealousy ("That other artist is more successful than me!"), envy ("That artist doesn't deserve their success because I'm better than them!"), anger ("I'll show those people who think I suck!") and self-hatred ("I suck. I need to work harder so I'll suck less."). All these negative motivators lead to corrosion of the spirit and often, a halt in work altogether. Appall your inner Business Manager with one mocha too many before you give in to any of these voices. You might never break even, but at least you'll save your soul.

Your Turn!

Here comes the fun one. Let's talk about ways to re-invig-orate yourself af-ter the onset of ennui! Here are some questions you can an-swer to choose your next incen-tive for slogging through your work:

STUFF THAT WOULD MOTIVATE ME... THAT SHOULD BE FUN TO COME UP WITH...

1. Are there any old pieces that had good bones but horrible execution? That you could definitely do better this time? Go through them and see if there are any just begging to be remodeled at your current skill level!

2. Are there any tools you've been hoping to try but haven't had a chance to? A piece of software? A new medium? A new venue! If you can't afford to go for it, at least do the research to see what it would take to give it a try.

3. Is there a (relatively harmless!) reward you could use as a ritual for having completed some measure of progress? Maybe it's sitting outside for a while and listening to the birds. Or a chance to play a favorite app without guilt? How about a plate of fresh fruit? (Okay, who are we kid-ding. Chocolate. Coffee. Fancy tea. The thing that floats your boat and that, in moderation, won't kill you!)

Business for the Right-Brained

4. Are there artistic peers you could hang out with? (Important: try to find some peers who are at around the same level of career you are, as this minimizes issues with envy and inability to commiserate on similar problems.) Sometimes, hanging out with friends who get you is a great incentive! If you don't live near any, and are tired of online socializing, maybe you can plan a physical get-together at some point—something to look forward to!

5. What other ways can you think of to pat yourself on the back for working in the face of adversity?

This is by far the most fun exercise of the bunch. I encourage you to think of returning to it to add new things as . . . incentive! For doing the other worksheets!

Know Thyself
(and Have a Plan)

ONE OF THE MOST ESSENTIAL assets you have going into business is a solid understanding of yourself: what you want to accomplish and what kind of work methods agree with you. So let's talk about. . . .

The Plan

Without a plan, any successes you have are going to be accidental and hard to reproduce. And there's nothing Business Manager and Marketer hate more than accidental, non-reproducible successes. Heck, Artist doesn't like them much either when you explain that she can't eat chocolate or buy art supplies that way.

Creating a business plan for your art career requires something most of us Artists love to do anyway: navel-gaze. So here are some questions you must answer to make one. You'll need input from all your selves to answer these, and you must be brutally honest. There's a niche for every artist, but unless you're honest about your answers you're going to wind up someplace you don't fit and then wonder later why you can't make it work.

The Plan Questionnaire

1. Do I like working with other people? Do I like getting out and chatting with them, or do I prefer to spend most of my time by myself?

2. Do I like experimenting with other people's ideas or do I prefer to work on my own ideas?

3. Do I work better with deadlines? If so, do I respond to deadlines I set for myself, or only those by other people?

4. How good am I at keeping to a schedule? If I set a schedule, can I keep to it?

5. How quickly do I coast to a stop without something prodding me (other people, external motivators like praise or money, etc)?

6. What kind of things keep me going and where do those things come from?

Business for the Right-Brained

7. What kind of art do I like to do, and who do I think it appeals to?

8. Do I need a steady, predictable income or can I handle irregular sums at irregular intervals?

9. What ways do I enjoy making my work available? You can tell this by seeing what things make you happiest to make and what kind of things you make most frequently.

Let's take some examples. Say you hate dealing with people, you really don't like implementing their ideas and you don't really like schedules or deadlines. Your studio is your haven, and you like to withdraw to it and put dreams on paper, beautiful intricate miniatures. If this workstyle makes you happy, drawing a web-comic is going to drive you insane. You should be trying to market yourself as a collectible fine artist and see about placing your work in galleries or selling it online where your interaction with others will be minimal.

But say you love using your skill to explore other people's ideas; you get high on being given a description of something you would never have thought of yourself and trying to make it real for them. You love their gasp of delight when they receive it . . . you love how it stretches your abilities. If you sit down at a table to come up with things on your own, you inevitably spend days doing . . . nothing. Your head feels empty. If this describes you, you shouldn't be trying to come up with ways to "think of your own ideas like other people do." You should be doing commissions and illustrative assignments, as many as you can handle.

Put these two artists in each other's work-environments and they will be miserable and make no money. But reverse them and they will be happy and productive. That's why knowing your work-style is so important and why honesty is crucial in evaluating your skills, interests and abilities.

The catch? Sometimes you don't know the answers to these questions until you experiment. Even worse, sometimes your preferences change from year to year. You have to keep on top of the changes by revisiting these questions regularly . . . or when you're miserable and don't know why.

Once you have described your work-style, you can ask Marketer to start brainstorming products and that would allow you to play to your strengths. Your marketing opportunities are mostly limited by your imagination and energy level. If you are willing to produce something, there's usually a way to sell it.

Business for the Right-Brained

Time Management

One of the other major skills necessary to a working artist—or a living human being, really—is figuring out how to manage your time. In the first chapter I described three roles. Even though these roles exist within your same person, they all need time to do their work. Business Manager needs time to do accounting and buy supplies and mail things and go to the bank and organize files. Marketer needs time to do research, analyze trends and respond to customers. And Artist, of course, has to produce art. Somehow you have to slice up the time your single physical body has to meet the needs of the three voices in your head.

Your first task when doing time management is to calculate how many hours a day you have to devote to your business. Be honest about this (you'll notice the repeating theme here). If you *could* work right up until bedtime, but doing so invariably makes it hard to fall asleep because you're still vibrating, cut that hour before bed and give it back to "relaxing so I can sleep" time. Be honest in the other direction too: if you're serious about this and you currently use your lunchhour for surfing, then take half an hour or the entire hour back and give it to your business.

Once you have a number of hours per week, it's time to decide how to split your time. There are two approaches to time management.

Static

Using this scheme, you take the amount of time you have and split it into chunks and do the same activities at the same time, every day, every week. You use the first free half hour to answer email and do research. You spend the next three hours producing your art. You spend the last hour of your day doing accounting/running errands. Whatever works for you, but you make a schedule and you stick with it.

The pros of this approach?

- It frees up the mental cycles you'd ordinarily be using for scheduling and gives them back as productive time. There's a reason routine is so celebrated; we tend to respond well to it.

- You can post "business hours." Patrons and customers like knowing when they can expect you to be available. If you can only respond to email once a week, but your website says that you answer email on Thursdays and you stick to that, you'll get a far more positive response than if you try to answer more frequently but erratically.

- Business hours also keep you from burning out. When we get excited, we have a tendency to overdo things. We neglect family or chores or the day job or friends and then wonder why we feel so wasted. If you know for a fact that you stop working at 8:30 PM so you can have family time and wind-down-for-bed time, then you won't run yourself into the ground. Exhausted Artists produce no work.

The cons? This is the most obvious one.

There will be times when the Artist doesn't care what your posted business hours are. She's going to do the work because she's on fire and you're just going to handle everything else while she's busy. Since your business involves sharing this excitement with your patrons, it's a bad idea to step on the Artist when she's burning to work. If you even can. I don't know about you, but mine won't stand down for anything. This leads us to the second approach to time management.

Dynamic

Your other choice is to take your available hours per week and split them according to whatever's going on. If you have a lot of accounting to do, throw yourself at that until it's done. If you have a deadline, put all your time toward that project. If you have an opportunity to go to a book fair or convention to do research, spend your weekend doing so.

The pros to this approach:

- You are far more flexible. You can respond to opportunities and challenges when they happen.

- You can accommodate a very temperamental and inspirational inner Artist.

- You get bored less easily.

- If your workstyle changes or you find your business is flagging, you can change your approach immediately to see if that helps.

The cons:

- You have to spend a lot more time scheduling, which eats into your productive time.

- It's easier to "not have time" for tasks you don't enjoy, which means that work piles up until it becomes almost impossibly daunting.

- You will have a tendency to mistake a problem that would respond to more time by taking time away from it. Many business problems can be solved only by doing the same things over and over again until you reach a critical mass of *something*: customers, inventory, buzz. If you're used to dynamic allocation of time, you might think "it's not working,

I'd better do something else" when the exact opposite approach is necessary.

For some people, a static approach is the only way to go: it keeps them at their desks and frees their mind from the burdens of constantly *thinking* about when they should be doing something. For others, dynamic is the only choice, because otherwise they'll feel stifled and resentful. For a lot of us, I suspect the best approach is a blend: do a little static scheduling to make sure you do certain tasks regularly, while leaving the rest of your hours more flexible. Your time management strategy might also change as your life situation and business needs change.

Later in this book we'll devote an entire chapter to why time management's so hard for all of us. But you need to know the practical details to form your plan.

Case Studies

So let's have a look at a few people.

The Full-Time Artist

Amalthea likes to make delicate brooches out of antique doilies and collage material in her spare time after work. She loves people and has a broad circle of friends and acquaintances with whom she likes to have coffee. One day one of them admires the brooch she's wearing and asks where she got it. When Amalthea tells her, "I make them," her friend encourages her to sell them.

The idea of selling her work through a dealer or online does not appeal to Amalthea, who likes excuses to get together with people. She also doesn't want the overhead of going to craft fairs or conventions. Instead, she thinks about book clubs and decides she likes the "intimate gathering" model. She rents a room at a local clubhouse, brings her coffee-maker and some baked goods and puts her work on the table, then invites her friends. They get together to talk. Some of them look at the jewelry; one of them buys a brooch.

Within a few months, Amalthea's friends are inviting their friends, who are coming for the coffee and conversation and leaving with jewelry. Pretty soon, she's selling more than enough of her brooches to cover her costs and make some pin money on the side. She thinks about expanding, but finds she doesn't like the thought of losing the intimate vibe of her "brooch salons."

One day an acquaintance asks her advice on putting together a bracelet, and Amalthea is happy to advise her. Her acquaintance is so pleased with her advice that she tells a friend that Amalthea is helpful (and also successful). They approach Amalthea with more questions, which she answers. In doing so, she discovers she likes to teach . . . and decides to offer classes on jewelry-making. She rents the same room as she did for her brooch salons, but fills it this time with paying students.

Teaching jewelry-making is fun and more lucrative than selling her brooches. Amalthea finds she can quit her day job and do nothing but teach. She still makes brooches for herself or for occasional sale.

In this example, we see that Amalthea has taken stock of (and been honest about) her principal strength: she likes people. Her initial business model takes advantage of that by maximizing her exposure to them; not only does this sell her work more effectively by letting her speak for it, she also enjoys herself. Her initial outlay was high: the cost of renting the room and feeding her friends, along with materials for her jewelry. But she was able to see that returned because she played to her strengths. It also allowed her to spot a new opportunity with a higher return: teaching, which let her charge for every person who walked in the door, instead of taking a chance on someone buying something while there. Plus, teaching jewelry-making sells her jewelry by spreading her reputation . . . and her jewelry sells her teaching, by enticing people already interested in hand-made jewelry to her classes.

The Part-Time Musician

Schmendrick is a quiet man who likes to make music in his attic, alone. He is currently unemployed. He doesn't like performing in front of people, but he is inspired by them; he likes to write music about his favorite stories. He has few friends and acquaintances, but what few he has are steadfast and true. It's one of these friends who encourages him to make some money off his art, if only to pay the electric bill.

Dealing with people exhausts Schmendrick, so his friend offers to help him set up a website where people can download his music for a few dollars a song.

Schmendrick offers some free samples. His costs are low (having already bought his musical instruments a long time ago, and using his computer to make the recordings), but he also makes little money. The thought of marketing himself more does not appeal to him, even if (as his friend says) he could make more money that way.

But he does like making music based on other people's work. So he decides, hesitantly, to contact a few of his favorite writers and ask if they're interested in him writing music for their stories. Most of them don't get back to him, but one of them sends him a delighted email. They begin a collaboration that results in a new novel from the author and a new album from Schmendrick. This album does well for Schmendrick, since the author's fans check him out. It works well for the author too, who loves the music and gets a lot of marketing material for free . . . songs he can use for book trailers, or play on podcasts. He decides to work with Schmendrick again.

Schmendrick enjoys this experience so much that he tries contacting a few more artists and authors to see if they're interested in collaborations. This time he mentions his previous collaboration with Author X . . . which brings him a few new artists willing to work with him. Pretty soon, Schmendrick is doing work with several artists and authors and enjoying himself immensely.

His friend encourages him to try playing at conventions where these authors attend. Schmendrick agrees to try, but he finds the experience stressful and does not want to repeat it.

A while later, Schmendrick finds a day job. He waffles over whether to take it, since he is making some money on his music now and could possibly make more. But he decides he doesn't like feeling the pressure to make art or starve, so he takes the day job and continues to work on his music on the weekends.

In this example, ruthless self-evaluation allowed Schmendrick to avoid some of the pitfalls of working as an artist in modern society: he was very clear about not wanting to deal with people or become a marketing or business expert. He liked doing a very specific kind of work: collaborations with other artists that let him write songs about stories that mattered to him. He did not like public performance or over-booking himself. So he made arrangements that allowed him to do this, and when given the choice between continuing to do it that way or trying to grow it as a business concern, he chose the former. This is not an easy decision, but sometimes it's the only decision.

Having a plan, figuring out how to allocate your hours and responding to changes in yourself and your environment: these things require as much creativity in many cases as making art. It's also the place that most artists trip up. You really have to identify your strengths, your weaknesses and what you're willing to do if you want to do business as an artist; self-deception leads to misery and failure. Often the reason artists lie to themselves about their strengths and weaknesses is because they've been told there's only one way to make it as an artist . . . but there's not. Each path to success is as individual as the person embarking on it, and only when you've been candid about what you're good at and what you're not can you find the path to your happy-art place.

The Day Job

A ND NOW, AN UNEXPECTED digression.

Sometimes I think all of us artists are born with That Dream. You know which. The one where we live in a golden studio or quaint cottage and do nothing but create. In That Dream, we wake up whenever we like, drift to our computers and guitars and paper and pass the day in a gentle fugue, creating as inspiration takes us. At the end of the month, money appears magically in our bank accounts and bills pay themselves, the better not to disturb our delicate artistic processes. If only we could achieve this dream, we think . . . we would finally be content.

We cling to the Dream as we slog through a dreary and mundane world where we have to work other jobs to pay those bills. We define our success as artists by whether we can realize it.

. . . and in so doing, we destroy ourselves.

Yes, you heard me right. The Dream is unrealistic and it fosters an attitude that sabotages us as artists. Day jobs aren't evil. They are not signs of failure. Believing that it must be one thing or the other—doing art or being a "wage-slave" or a "corporate drone"—is a false dichotomy. It's time to let it go.

FIRST: Reality

Let's begin by killing the sacred cow: our fantasy about being a full-time artist. When we move to full-time artist status, we don't leave the work world, we simply change venues. Art becomes our work.

And oh, what work it is. Money doesn't appear in our accounts because we decide to devote ourselves to our talents, it must be earned . . . and we're the ones who have to go out and convince people to give it to us. We're the ones who book the venues, investigate opportunities, do the accounting. We pay the bills, curse at our taxes, read the contracts . . . and then go to the library to check out books on the contracts so we can make sure we understood what we just read. We spend as much—maybe more—time in marketing and finance as we do actually making things . . . and when we make things we can no longer afford to wait for inspiration. We have to develop ways to deal with the downtimes and power through them.

In our fantasies, a full-time artist's area of responsibility narrows to a single, manageable task: to do art, the thing we enjoy, that fulfills us. But in reality, a full-time artist's responsibilities expand to fill all available space, and there is no one else to help shoulder them. We pay our own insurance, issue our own paychecks, manage our own sick and vacation time. And if there's no money for payroll this month, we're the ones to blame . . . and we're the ones who go home poor.

But wait! You say. What about hiring people to do these tasks for you? Then you really can do nothing but your art!

To that I say: you're absolutely correct. Some artists will make enough money to afford promoters, publishers, agents, accountants, publicity managers, administrative assistants and a cleaning service so they don't have to dust their own keyboards. I'm pretty sure you're going to have to be a rock-star artist to pay someone else to do all these tasks for you so you can concentrate on your art. Do you want to give up art entirely just because you don't win the fame-and-fortune lottery?

M.C.A. Hogarth

But let's talk about that whole "concentrating on your art thing." Because that's the key to the whole problem.

SECOND: Growth. Ours.

You remember that new author that you thought was so brilliant? Her first book was amazing and you couldn't wait for the second, and the second was amazing too. You weren't the only person who thought so . . . and you were happy when the bio on the back of the book talked about how she was going to start writing more now that she could afford to do nothing but write. The third book was great. The fourth too.

But by the fifth book, something was wrong. The sixth was even more lackluster. They're making her write too fast, you thought. (But wasn't that the point of her doing nothing but writing? So she could deliver the goods to her fans more often?) Maybe it was that her editors were no longer brave enough to take a red pen to her manuscripts. (But even editors can only work with what they're given.)

You didn't buy the seventh book. You picked up the tenth to see if something had changed and put it down halfway through and the words in your head were: "She's writing the same story over and over again."

. . .

That ringing silence? That's us coming face to face with one of our secret fears. We don't want to become That Author who can't seem to escape the same story. The Painter whose work ten years later looks so much like the work he did ten years before that you could buy a single painting and own his entire oeuvre. The Band whose 50-year-old members are still singing songs that were authentic when they were angry teens but sound ridiculous from gray-haired grandparents.

We don't want to become That Artist. The only way to avoid it is to live a life. Not the life you planned, and not the life of a recluse in a garret. But a life full of bumps, bruises and experiences you might have preferred never to go through.

And the fastest, easiest and cheapest way to get those experiences is a Day Job.

You Have Got to Be Kidding Me

I'm not. I'm totally serious. That your Day Job may give you some measure of financial freedom is secondary to its effect on you as an artist. A lot of people ask me how to stay inspired, how to keep the well from drying up. The answer is right here, right now, in your seemingly mundane life, because something is mundane only as far as we let it be. We are transformers of experience; we are lenses through which the unassuming and the unexamined are illuminated. When you have to get up every morning and go somewhere and deal with people and solve problems and beat your head against stupidity and triumph over unexpected challenges . . . that's when you have something to say.

But wait! You say. You have got be kidding. How is that going to be of interest to anyone? My life as a drive-through Starbucks barista? My life in a cubicle?

And to that I say: your life as a barista, a cubicle-drone, a real estate agent, a parent, an inventory manager, a coder . . . all those things are more interesting than your life as a

cloistered artist. Because most people can't relate to your life as a cloistered artist, but a lot of them are going to understand those other things. Your take on them will let them see their own lives in a new way. Maybe a more productive one. And that leads us to . . .

THIRD: Growing an Audience.

One of the most common patterns I see in the "back-of-the-book" bios of successful artists is an incredibly eclectic biography. These are people who've been long-haul truckers, waitresses, managers; flipped burgers, rewritten process documents, sold antiques; they've been consultants and survey takers and every conceivable job, and a lot of them have done six or seven or nine of them and are experimenting with #10. It's not because they're inherently flaky. It's because Artists are interested in everything . . . or they can find something about everything to be interested in. And this is the power that intrigues people.

A lot of people ask me how you can broaden your audience, thinking that it's Marketing alone that attracts people, and while it's true that a good Marketing campaign can draw people it's the *Artist* who will keep them. It's when you broaden your life experience that you broaden your audience: not just the drive-by visitors, but the patrons who'll stay with you year after year. Because let's face it: the people most interested in a cloistered artist's life are . . . other artists. If you want to attract enough people to actually succeed, you need to speak to more than your peers.

An artist who hasn't lived will be relevant to very few people. It sounds crazy and paradoxical, but the Day Job often leads to success as an artist because it gives you a life to react to and things to say.

Wait, Are You Saying We Should Never Be Full-time Artists?

No, but I am saying that being a full-time artist, in addition to not being like the Dream, comes with an unexpected challenge: you have to find a way to duplicate the unpredictability of a life outside your studio. And frankly, a lot of us can't . . . or won't. Left to ourselves, we fall naturally onto the path of least resistance. We don't like subjecting ourselves to unnecessary suffering, to boredom, to uncomfortable situations. We grow accustomed to routine. We like it. And breaking ourselves out of that mold requires discipline and imagination.

It can be done: you can drag yourself out of the office. You can take classes. You can attend parties and openings, do charity work, get involved in the community. You can keep learning. But unsurprisingly, in addition to requiring a lot of energy and imagination to plan, doing these things on your own often costs money. Sometimes a lot of money. The Day Job, on the other hand, will continually expose you to experiences both salutary and frustrating . . . and make money! It's as if you're being paid to be inspired! And then you can turn around and spend that money on your supplies, or on experiences you actually want to have (like that martial arts class you've been eyeing, or that parachute jump that will change your life).

Squeeeeee

Adjusting Our Attitudes

The modern artist can never be happy. If she's not miserable because she can't avoid a Day Job, then she's miserable because working as a full-time artist was not the easy fantasy she was craving. The only solution to this problem is to realize that a Day Job can be and often is a great blessing; and full-time art is not always the right choice (and is never the easy one). Instead of clinging to the dichotomy of Artist-versus-Drone, aim instead for a textured life, one where Day Jobs and Full-Time Art interweave as your financial situation and artistic needs drive you.

But wait! This is all very philosophical, Jaguar. And not at all practical. It's not like you at all!

You're right, and I'm going to talk about the practicalities next. But without covering this very important attitude shift, none of it will matter. Your resentment of your Day Job and your persistent feelings of failure will drain you faster than any job ever could. No suggestion will help you if you don't let go of the idea that doing anything but art is awful, like being sentenced to Hell.

Art is not something you do instead of life. It's something you do *because* of it.

So, having discussed the philosophical reasons why thinking of the Day Job as the opposite of Art is bad, let's move on to some pragmatics.

Mindsets for Success

First, unless you have a secondary passion (say, you feel strongly about libraries and would be happy being a librarian), resist the urge to treat your Day Job as a career. Your family and peers may accuse you of lack of ambition if you aren't scrabbling up the corporate ladder, but you only need as much money as keeps you comfortable. There is no dishonor in flipping a burger if you do it well and come home ready to dive into your other projects. Seriously: don't lose sight of this or you may find yourself CFO of some random technology firm working 90 hour weeks, wondering what happened and how you ended up here. Your object is not money for its own sake. Your object is a little financial stability and a reason to get out of the studio.

Second, think of your day job as a choice. Most of us aren't used to this idea; when you're down to your last penny you're not supposed to *choose*, you're supposed to take what you can get. Allow yourself the radical notion that you should look for the job that's right for you. You might not find it immediately, but don't give up experimenting until you've found the one that works.

Finding the Right Day Job

Everyone's right Day Job is going to be different depending on their art and workstyle. I can't tell you how to find that Right Job. I can, however, enumerate a couple of common pitfalls:

- **The Day Job That's Too Much Like Your Art:** You draw. You take a job as a graphic artist. You spend all day at the office drawing what other people tell you to . . . and come home not wanting to even *look* at a piece of paper. If this is your problem, find a day job that has nothing to do with your art!

- **The Day Job That Leaves You Physically Exhausted:** You spend ten hours a day restocking shelves. You come home, faceplant and wake up the next morning to do it again. Art requires some physical energy. If this is your problem and you can't cut back on your hours, it's time to look for a new job.

- **The Day Job That Leaves You Mentally Exhausted:** You spend all day behind a retail counter dealing with irritating customers. When you come home, all you can do is watch TV and go to bed. Mental exhaustion is just as big a problem as physical. If you can't cut back on your hours, again . . . it's time to hunt for some new job.

Business for the Right-Brained

Some styles of Day Job to consider:

- **The Day Job That Gives You Time to Think:** If you need time to work out things in your head, consider taking a day job that involves physical labor. You can massage your clients while working out your next story, or do landscaping while pondering that song that just won't come together.

- **The Day Job That Expects You to Sit at a Computer:** You can do a lot of useful things at a computer on your time off, even if your art form doesn't necessarily need a computer, like writing. If you end up with a day job that puts you in a cubicle, consider using your spare cycles/lunch breaks to catch up on business emails, do social networking or work on marketing or ad materials. (Phones are another good thing to have access to; you can use your lunch breaks to catch up on business calls on your cellphone.)

- **The Day Job That Gets You In Front of People:** If you're not good with people and want practice dealing with them, the Day Job that makes you interact with them is a great way to learn strategies for customer care. Every interaction is an opportunity! Take notes!

- **The Day Job That Gives You Ideas:** If you're low on ideas and want to bulk up on them, consider finding a way-out-there job, something you'd never think to do. Work as a medical transcriptionist, a legal aide, a travel agent. If you can't think up a weird job like this, head to the library or local bookstore and consult their career section: there are entire books dedicated to jobs you might not think of, everything from wedding planning to manning tollbooths.

Some Examples

Day Jobs are as varied as the artists who work them. I've known an actress who worked as a nanny, a job that allowed her more freedom to schedule auditions; a musician who did data entry at home so he could sleep in after long practice sessions; an office assistant who wrote short stories during her lunch hours. I've met *three* visual artists who worked at framing shops so they could borrow the equipment after hours to frame their own work, at least two jewelers who owned or worked at bead shops, a part-time barista who was attending art school on the side and more people than I can count who worked 8-to-5 jobs in cubicles so they could afford to experiment with things that might or might not pan out.

Above all, your #1 strategy: if the job isn't working for you, start looking for a new one. This Day Job is not your career. Your goal is to make enough money to free yourself from some (or all) of your financial anxieties and to get out of the studio . . . not to chain yourself to a miserable existence. Remember the mindsets: I am not my Day Job, and I am allowed to choose the work I do. Arm yourself with these realizations and keep looking until you find the right fit.

But Wait!

Am I saying that all Day Job problems can be solved by . . . finding a new one?

Why yes. I am.

But wait! That's crazy! Not everyone can just up and find a new job! Some people have financial situations that make that impossible. Some people have physical limitations that make their job prospects poor!

You're right. Sometimes we'll have to stick it out in jobs that we dislike or can't easily escape. Sometimes that problem is untenable. But often, our problem is that we become comfortable in that routine. It gets hard to find the energy to look for something new. We get used to the idea of being trapped.

The moment you start thinking that, you close the cage door on yourself.

As artists, our calling is to make art. This is our passion, our purpose. Our Day Jobs are side-lines. We can't afford to be attached to them if they bar us from our purpose, which means we have to be ready to let go of them if they get in the way. If you find yourself mired in a Day Job that keeps you from working, but that you have to keep for practical reasons, you have only two choices: find a new one, or learn to work despite it. Both these choices are hard but you have to make one of them, or you'll renege on that joy that is your birthright. Never let go of the possibility of finding a new Day job. And if you can't . . .

Your Story

. . . then it's time to write your story. The one where the world tried to crush you and you didn't let it. The one where you triumphed against all adversity to eke out one or two pieces of art when you had a spare moment, because to not do so would be giving in. And *you don't give in.* Ever. Not if it means giving up the art.

If you're trapped and there's no way out, if your quest for a different job isn't bearing fruit, if you have no other choice, the only choice you can make is to be the Artist Who Didn't Let the Bastards Grind Her Down. Turn your anger and resentment into power and use them for fuel. Bring a notebook small enough for a pocket with you and jot down ideas in stolen time. Skip lunch to write. Stay up late after everyone's asleep to get in ten minutes of work before you collapse. Do it again the next day because ten minutes day after day adds up. Tell yourself the story every morning you wake up: "I'm the hero who can't be kept down." Tell it to yourself until you believe it.

(And then, find a new job the moment you can.)

Addendum to the Story

. . . did you notice that the Story is another mindset? Training yourself to succeed, to think of yourself as someone with choices, to think of your Day Job itself as an asset to your art . . . all these are the most powerful tools you have in your arsenal as an artist. All the time-management strategies in the world, all the coping tactics, the plans, all of them will come to nothing if you don't have the mindsets firmly in place first. With the right attitude nothing is going to stop you. Without it, you'll only get where you want to go by accident . . . if you get there at all.

The Personal Jaguars

- Manning a help desk taught me the importance of self-control (boy howdy, was that a story!) and gave me a chance to develop a customer "face."

- Working in web design taught me how to make my first website. And then my next. And my next . . .

- When I went into process analysis and development, I learned how important processes are to efficient workflow, and took that knowledge to my workflow as an artist.

- When I did business analysis, I learned things about trending, tracking and statistics that are serving me even now as I do marketing for my art.

- Working in Product Marketing taught me about customer care and how to deal with faulty products and botched customer relationships.

- Inventory control gave me the opportunity to experiment with project management and the importance of annotating and filing *everything*.

- Working at a university gave me a chance to practice handling sudden gluts of work, exposed me to the breadth of people's ideas, and allowed me to take classes for free, resulting in a lot of drawings about medical ethics.

- My work as a massage therapist gave me endless fodder for blog columns, illustrations and observations about people.

- My stint as a technical writer taught me the importance of

Business for the Right-Brained

brevity in communication, which led to my first flash fiction collections.

- Sidelining my Day Jobs for parenting has changed me so much I can't begin to enumerate the things I'm learning, and all of them are affecting my work as an artist.

I have never had a Day Job that didn't teach me something I couldn't turn around and take to my art, even the ones that sent me home physically and mentally exhausted, even the ones that slowed my production down to trickles. I'm hoping that the philosophies and mindsets I've discussed in this chapter will help you find something of value in your Day Job too . . . because the truth is that most of us will need a Day Job for part or even most of our lives as artists. But we're not defined by the "hobby" that pays for our real jobs, and if you take away anything from the Day Job chapter, that's the message: you will always be an artist, no matter what you do with the rest of your life. Count on it.

Metrics, Part 1: Tracking

During one of my Day Job stints, I was asked to put together metrics so management could gauge the performance of our technicians. Specifically, they asked for a Mean Time to Repair figure; they wanted to focus their performance objectives around shortening the length of time it took to fix customer issues. Obediently I went out, collected statistics and started generating graphs that were posted every month on the call center wall.

The result? MTTR started trending downward . . . and customer complaints skyrocketed. Management's decision that time was the sole indicator of success caused our technicians to close tickets as fast as possible, even if they did a poor job of fixing the issues. Quality went out the window, but at least we were delivering bad customer service really quickly!

Success in business is not a matter of a single measurement. Like my poor call center colleagues, you can flog yourself with a single metric and still end up failing. As the joke went in the department (and everywhere else I did business analysis and performance reporting), you get more of what you measure for, and what you choose to measure often defines—and limits—the parameters of your success.

Art no less than any other concern benefits from proper tracking and trend analysis. In this chapter, we will cover what kinds of things you can track to avoid limiting yourself or failing to spot important problems or opportunities; and then, in the chapter following, we'll discuss how to use those statistics to keep a thumb on the pulse of your business.

Tracking

The four major categories you want to track in order to understand how you're doing are Money, Time, People and Products. As you settle into your groove as a working professional you may find other (often more specific) categories, but as a baseline, you gotta have these four. Let's have a look, then.

Money.

The most obvious of our categories is money: money in (revenue), money out (expenses) and profit (revenue - expenses).

That means we want to know how much money people have paid us for our art; much money we've spent to make, market and sell our art; and whether the former is greater

Business for the Right-Brained

than the latter. Compiling these numbers will give you a narrow but implacable view of your bottom line: are you making money or losing it? And by how much?

Please note! You must be absolutely rigorous in your money-tracking. If you have a friend who's willing to be your agent to a specific show "for free," but in reality you will end up buying him lunch or making him cookies, then you keep that receipt or that grocery bill. Your "free" trip to that show might actually be costing you $10-20.

So, the basics of what you should be tracking for income:

• **Date.** Should be everywhere, on everything.

• **Price.** This is the amount you charged the customer.

• **Actual Amount In.** Some portion of your sales will be subject to sales tax (and you should know which, and how much you pay based on country, state and county). Similarly, depending on how you were paid, some of your money will get eaten by transaction fees: merchant fees to accept credit cards, commissions, Paypal surcharges, etc. You absolutely must keep track of these things or they will erode your earnings out from under you.

• **What was it for?** What product did you sell, or sell a piece of? Was it a print? An original? A song download?

• **Who bought it?** Customer name goes here! More on customers later, under People.

As you develop your business, you might find additional things to track. For instance, I track the type of payment, with the possibilities being "tip," "royalties," "payment," and "layaway." This helps me see how much of my business is based on straight sales of merchandise versus tips versus people buying items on plans versus passive income streams.

Basics of what you should be tracking for expenses:

- **Date.** You get the idea on this being on everything.

- **Amount out.** Again, this is what you paid to buy whatever it is you need.

- **Actual amount out.** In some cases, you should be able to get state tax exemptions. Look up your local laws or talk to an accountant about this.

- **What did you buy?** Be both general and specific: put in a category for the expense and detail what it actually was.

- **Where did you get it?** Where you bought it, in detail enough that you could find the place, call them or use them again.

- **Tax Categories.** It will save you time come tax-time if you look up the expense categories for your country/state's income tax and tag each expenses as it comes in.

Important: Save your receipts and invoices! Proof of transactions is handy. Keep a file folder or enveloped labeled with the year and put all your receipts in it in the order they accrue. It will probably make your life easier to have separate folders for expenses versus income (sales receipts and invoices).

Time.

Creation (the Art Side). Contrary to what movie montages would have the general public think, we know that making art takes time. Sitting down and pushing a painting from sketch to completion may be the work of 40 hours, spread over several months; completing a novel might take us six months of writing an hour a day. Polishing a piece of music, putting together a piece of jewelry, sewing a corset or stuffed animal . . . from the moment you sit down to work to the moment you get up and call it a day, you should be logging how much time you spend. Literally: right now, go grab a pen and paper and jot it down. Or make a spreadsheet. Keep a database, whatever works for you. Note not just the time, but what you were working on.

Important: don't just log the passage of time, log the exact working time. If you spend six hours on a piece of art over two weeks, write down the six hours, as well as the two weeks. One metric will tell you how long something actually takes; the other will help you measure the efficiency of your work schedule.

Your goal, measuring your work as an artist: to have a record of how long specific projects take you, and to be able to estimate in the future how long similar ones will take you.

Marketing and Selling. Preparation for sale also takes time, whether that preparation involves framing, editing and mailing to an agent, recording a studio version or boxing your work up and mailing it somewhere. When we go to fairs, gigs, conventions and gallery openings, we are spending time on our business. When we hike to the post office to mail things, spend an hour on the phone with a client solidifying details for a commission, or lose a frustrating evening to an attempt to fix a broken tool, we are spending time on our business.

This is a place a lot of us trip. Logging your time-per-project is a lot easier than logging your time spent on marketing and selling . . . but logging your marketing/selling time is *critical.* Every hour you spend preparing your work for sale is time you aren't spending making art, so you have to make it count—more on that in our Trending segment next week.

Your goal, measuring your work as a marketer: to know how long it takes you to productize anything, so that if you run out of something you can immediately turn around and tell the next customer, "I can get that to you in [x] days." You also want these statistics later so you can decide whether a specific product based on a piece of art is worth your time.

People.

Your third tracking category involves people, a category we can split into two halves. First, your audience: your visitors, your customers (people who buy from you once or twice) and your patrons (people who are consistent buyers of your work). And second, your networking and business contacts.

JUST PASSIN' THROUGH. NOTHIN' TO SEE HERE.

HMM. I LIKED THE FIRST ONE... MAYBE I'LL LIKE THE SECOND ONE TOO?

MOAR PLZ!!

THE THREE CUSTOMERS

Audience.

You'll notice immediately that separating your audience into Patron, Customer and Visitor categories requires you to know how often they've bought from you and whether they were looking . . . not necessarily an easy statistic to gather. In fact, visitors may be the hardest statistic to pinpoint. You can make some educated guesses at it by tracking website hits, offering guestbooks at physical locations, or collecting comments from people on websites or fan emails . . . but those really are estimations, and you're never going to be completely sure how many people glanced at your work somewhere. Even if you count out a stack of (say) 50 business cards and postcards and set them out at a fair, counting them when you go home will tell you how many people were interested enough to take one, but not necessarily how many people came in and had a look.

(I do recommend that you never send out advertising materials without counting them, and requesting that the remainder be packed and sent back so you can gauge interest.)

So your goal with customers is to get visitors to give you their names (or some evidence of their interest), and then to convert them into customers, and perhaps later, patrons.

What you need to know:

- **Who They Are.** Your first sale should net you some basic information on your customer: name, address, email address, possibly phone number. That's enough for the one or two-time buyers. Once people start edging into patron status, the amount of information you have on them should increase. You should make an effort to get to know them and their interests: have they mentioned that they'd like to make costumes out of your fashion design? Did they tell you they wore your necklace to a charity event (and what charity was it, if they said)? Did they mention giving your book to their kids? Do you even know how many kids they have? You have a relationship with patrons that requires more reciprocation on your part. You should be able to send them birthday greetings (with a coupon) as well as contact them when you complete a work that meets their tastes. Which brings us to . . .

- **Buying Habits.** What are your customers buying? How often? Do you have a customer who only buys your memoirs and eschews your fiction? Or a patron who'll pick up every $5 postcard you offer, but doesn't buy larger prints? Do you have customers who never spend more than $20 per item? Or customers who never buy unless you're offering a sale? Which is also related to . . .

- **Crossover Customers.** If you do multiple kinds of work (say, you're a writer-jeweler), do you have clients who buy both your writing and your jewelry? Or are your audiences mostly separate?

Networking Contacts.

You head out to a convention, get invited to a party, and end up chatting with some senior art director, who hands you a business card. Later, you send email with a portfolio to that art director . . . who refers you to her assistant. Who signs you up for a big project.

Keeping track of business contacts is important. They come in two sorts:

- **Possible Contacts.** Someone tells you about someone who works as an editor. You find an agent's business card at a local gallery. You look up a list of reputable business managers and take down some names and numbers. Possible contacts are people you haven't met but that you'd like to. You should always keep an eye peeled for people with whom you could pursue a business interest to your mutual advantage, hoping to turn them into . . .

- **Personal Contacts.** That senior art director you were sharing a beer with. A distributor one of your mutual friends introduced you to. An editor you shared a convention panel with, and hit it off with. Personal contacts are people who might remember your name if you contact them with a proposal.

Some things you should track with business contacts:

- **Basic contact information.** Name, business, email, physical address and phone number if you have it. Preferred method of address: if you overheard that Marketing VP Elizabeth prefers to be called 'Liza', put that down somewhere. Likewise 'Ms.' versus 'Mrs.' and yes, gender too; some names are androgynous and you probably don't want to be making that mistake. Scratch that. You *definitely* don't want to be making that mistake.

- **How You Found Them.** Card picked up at some art show? Convention party?

- **Projects You Pitched Them.** Keep track of anything you've run by them, and whether they got picked up or not. This will give you a sense for the health of the connection: do the two of you have similar tastes? How likely is it that a new project sent their way will result in something concrete?

Important Note! Business contacts are no good to you unless you use them. While you shouldn't be pinging someone with an inappropriate proposal, like sending an art director seeking abstracts your newest representational portfolio, these people are in business: they're looking for opportunities, just like you. You should not be shy about sending them a query if you've got something they might be interested in. Here's a clue that you're being too shy: in your head, you hear phrases like these: "this might not exactly fit the letter of what they're looking for," "they probably have too many people submitting things" or the king of all BAD: "I don't want to bother them."

Burn those words out of your brain. You do not have the kind of personal relationship with your business contacts that would require you to fret about *bothering* them. (Unless they become good friends. Later.) This is what you owe them: politeness. Professional behavior. They may respond with an equally polite and professional 'no' to your proposal. This is not the end of the world, it won't burn your bridges with them. Regroup, keep moving, and if you come up with something that looks like a match for that person in the future, try again.

You are not chasing unicorns here. And even unicorns would be less fussy.

Products.

Finally, very finally: Products.

Why finally, when arguably Products are the basis of our business? Exactly because they are the basis of our business. They're going to show up on our Money tracking lists, associated with incoming money (or outgoing, for supplies). They're linked on our Time lists with creation and marketing. They show up again in People associated with customers who were interested in something and business contacts you might have used to advance them.

In short, your Products are intimately tangled with every other statistic in the group.

So, basic things you should keep track of with Products:

- **Art the Product is Based on.** If you write a story, the story name goes here. (How you sell it, as a physical novel, as a download, etc, goes in a different category.)

- **Type of Art.** If you do more than one kind of art, typing your project is essential. A writer might go with novel, short story, article, poem; an artist-musician with painting, album, song, etc. You will have to experiment to decide how this category will help you, even if that means later going back and re-tagging everything you've got records for.

- **Type of Product.** As discussed thoroughly in Chapter 2, your piece of art is not a product. Make sure you note what kind of product is selling so you'll have statistics about, say, whether posters sell better than postcards. Label anything that you sell discretely, whether it's a single-song download or a sketch.

- **Dates.** While the Time category will tell you how long it took you to finish something, it probably won't be telling you when you completed it. If you have any substantial body of work, knowing which products you issued in 1997 will probably be helpful.

- **Location.** If your work results in physical objects, knowing where you put them is helpful. Non-physical objects can probably be indicated by location on your hard drive.

Real World

If you're looking at this list of things to keep track of and thinking, 'Cripes, I'm going to miss something!' I have something to tell you:

You're absolutely right.

This is a lot to keep track of, particularly when you're starting out. You'll probably fall down on entire categories of statistics. The important part is to get back up and keep hacking at it. Maybe you'll be great on time estimation and really shabby at keeping track of people; maybe you'll remember the customers but not your business contacts; maybe you'll get the creative-time-per-project down before you get the marketing-time-per-project. At least you're getting *something*. As you get to be an old pro with the statistics you're comfortable with, branch out into the ones you've been neglecting. Eventually you'll get it all under control. Which brings us to . . .

A Note on Tools

You'll notice that the Jaguars have not suggested specific tools to get the job of tracking statistics done. Many people will prefer spreadsheets, some will want specialized financial software and still others are going to find an artist-specific package that meets their needs. Some of us will even do what I did one dumb day and write a web database application for it . . . and others are going to eschew computers completely and decide the best way to track things is with colored sticky notes on their wall.

Organizing your business records is not a minor topic, and is often very individual. I would encourage you to experiment with several different record-keeping methods until you find the one that works best for you. I find it handy to have the kind of sorting/math tools that come with a spreadsheet, but if you find it more intuitive to use a leather-bound ledger, absolutely do so. As long as you keep your records meticulously, the method doesn't matter. Some methods might entail more work on your part come time for trend analysis, but they can still do the job as long as you have the numbers.

And as always, be open to new tools. As your business grows or changes, your recording tools might have to change with it.

Metrics, Part 2: Trending

WE CONTINUE WITH PART 2 of Tracking and Trending, in which we use our statistics for the powers of good! Rustle up your lists, spreadsheets, sticky notes and databases and tell your inner Artist she'll get to put her apron back on and have fun later, it's time for some number-crunching!

Trending

So, you've set up a system. You're tracking money, time, people and products. What now?

Now . . . you look for patterns.

Let's say you've written a novel, a short story and an article, and all of them sold (lucky you!). First, you look at your Money statistics.

Novel: $5000.
Short Story: $250.
Article: $100.

From this perspective, the novel looks like the clear winner here. But we're not done with our statistics. Let's move on to Time.

Novel: 183 hours.
Short Story: 4 hours.
Article: 16 hours.

Wow, big difference here! So let's whip out the calculator and divide our Time by our Money. Doing that, we get a per-hour figure:

Novel: $27 an hour.
Short Story: $62.50 an hour.
Article: $6.25 an hour.

So, the short story actually gave you the greatest bang for the buck. But we have one more category to have a look at,

People.

Novel: 20,000 copies sold.
Short Story: 50 downloads.
Article: 5,000 circulation.

And now . . . we don't know what to think. If we want to reach the most customers, the obvious choice is the novel, with the article as the runner-up.

But wait! You were going to tell us how metrics were supposed to *help* us. How is confusing ourselves going to accomplish that?

Business Goals

Your key here is that you need to establish long-term and short-term business goals. Most of us will have 'make a profit' as a long-term business goal (and usually a specific amount we aim to earn a year). But to meet that long-term goal of profitability, we need to keep an eye on the issues that are preventing it. These problems will inform our short-term goals. Let's have a look at some examples.

Example 1: It's Simple

So you have a problem: you're not making enough money. Step one is to identify the nature of the problem, so you whip out your statistics.

Checking the Money category, you see that your expenses are higher than your revenue: you're spending more than you're earning. From that list you see the majority of your expenses involve traveling to fairs. You flip to the Revenue side of the sheet and start flagging all the sales you've made at fairs and see that you don't make enough at these fairs to cover your expenses. Double-checking your People list, you see that the customers you've gotten at fairs are mostly one-time buyers; you've only gotten one or two patrons from your efforts there. You don't see a lot of your advertising material walking away at these fairs, indicating that even your advertising is doing badly.

So your problem: you spend a lot of money to attend shows that neither make you a profit nor seem to result in broadening your customer base. Axe your show schedule for a year, spend your time on other projects and see what that does to your bottom line.

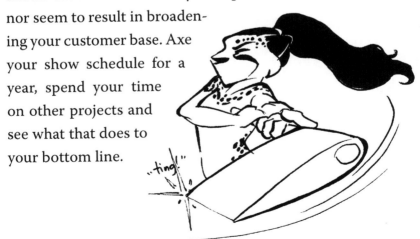

Business for the Right-Brained

Example 2: It's Complicated

Once again, you're not making enough money, and a look at your numbers. You see that your biggest expense involves traveling to fairs, so you check your Revenue . . .

. . . and your Revenue numbers indicate you make a lot of money at fairs. Most of it, in fact. Double-checking the People side of the equation, you see that you've found *all* of your patrons (except one!) at these fairs, and you're giving away a lot of advertising material. When you look at the Time statistics, you see that you spend a lot of time preparing for these fairs. You run the time-versus-money numbers and discover that it still looks good: the sales made to your patrons offset the cost and put you in the black.

So . . . your #1 expense is tied to your #1 profit-making activity, but you're still not making money. What's going wrong?

You settle down with a list of your other projects and run the time versus money on them. You discover that in almost every other arena you're spending way too much time to make almost-to-no money. When you check the customer listing, you see that these efforts have resulted in almost no customers acquired.

Your problem, then? You're spending too much time on activities extraneous to the ones that are really making your money. Spend a year doing nothing but shows (and expanding into new venues) and see if your profit number starts climbing.

But you don't have to use the numbers to troubleshoot problems. You can also use them for planning. For instance:

Example 3: Tooth Explosion

Things are looking pretty good for you when your dentist pops the bad news: that stabbing pain you've been mainlining aspirin for is an abscess. You need a $2000 root canal. You can cover some of that from your account, but you need to rustle up a good $500 of it, and soon, before your stomach lining bleeds off.

You check your statistics. Your goal is to find an activity that has earned you the most money for the least amount of preparatory time. Scanning the lists, you see that you have two possibilities. Posting a sale will often get you around the right amount of money in return for printing, packing and shipping time . . . you can do that. Or you can sell off a single original, which will get you around the right amount of money if someone wants to buy it. Flipping to your customer list, you see that several of your patrons haven't bought anything in a while, so they might be interested in something; in fact, you have (thoughtfully) notated next to one of them that he's always wanted the original for one particular image you've never sold.

You drum your fingers and think. The sale is going to take a lot more time to organize and manage, but it has a greater chance of making at least some return because it draws on many different people. The original, if you can sell it, will take care of all your problems immediately, but it will depend completely on whether one or two people are willing to buy. Plus, you're not sure you're ready to part with that particular image.

The post office is on the way to the oral surgeon. You start putting together the sale.

Example 4: Small Ponds

You're not making a bad living, but you're concerned: a lot of your money comes from the same pool of customers. If the economy dips too much, you'll take far too big a hit to your profit if those handful of customers see hard times. Since you're doing okay now, you decide it's a good time to start spending some time and money on broadening your customer base.

You check your People statistics and see that a lot of your customers seem to have come from local gigs. Checking the time and money ratios, you see this is somewhat costly, but it's worked for you before. You decide to spend some time researching new local gigs and checking for openings at the ones you've played before—you have a list of those already, with addresses and phone numbers. But you're concerned that you may already have used up the local market, so you decide it's time to expand elsewhere. You have almost no statistics on playing outside your immediate geographical zone, so you set aside a couple of days to do some research.

You find a few possibilities: there's a topical podcast you can try approaching, which will take only a few minutes for the query. There's an interesting new website that re-prices songs based on number of downloads, up to a cap you set: that looks especially promising, as for very little effort you might get some new listeners and a little money. And according to your spreadsheet you have a few patrons who are authors . . .

you decide to ask them if they'd like to use a song for a book trailer, to see if you can reach some of their audience.

All these endeavors will take time, and even if they make a little money they probably won't make enough to offset how much you'd earn by working on new music. But you decide that broadening your audience is more important to your long-term business goal of maintaining profitability than any short-term profit you'd make using the time some other way.

As you can see, keeping these metrics can be a powerful troubleshooting tool. But you don't have to use them solely when your business is failing . . .

Making a Habit of Tracking

To troubleshoot your business, you need to know how it's doing . . . which implies that you're keeping an eye on it. So how often should you check your statistics? And which ones should you be checking? Everyone's answer is going to vary depending on their personality. Some of you will find it tedious and want to touch it as infrequently as possible; some of you will find it fascinating and probably end up messing with it every week. Whichever camp you fall into, I would tender these suggestions as baseline:

- **Accounting**. Don't put off entering your sales and expenses. The longer you wait, the more work will build up and soon enough it will become a paperwork monster that you won't want to beard with a four-foot sword and a fully automatic Red Stapler of Doom. Keep your accounting manageable: record sales and expenses as you make them, or at least weekly.

- **Profit-Revenue-Expenses**. Check this at least monthly to see how you're doing and to make course corrections. If your profit is plunging, you don't want to wait half a year to notice; you want to use your statistics to try to identify the problem and fix it as soon as possible.

- **Big Events**. If you attend a large event, do the numbers as soon as you get back so you can see whether it was worth doing (and if it wasn't, how much you have to make up).

- **Customers**. Check this a few times a year to see if you've secured any new patrons so you can make plans on what special offers or thank-yous you'd like to make. At very least check once in fall to prepare for holiday sales and card exchanges.

Depending on your business, you'll find statistics you'll want to track for your own needs, edification or amusement. Some of you will track number of reviews, others newspaper mentions, some of you books sold per month. Don't be afraid to strike out and measure something seemingly frivolous if it's going to help you. If tracking the number of rejection letters you've gotten over the course of your career spurs you to submit more work, by all means, track the letters!

When Statistics Meet Reality

But wait! Doesn't all this measuring, planning, pattern-matching assume an ideal world? That you'll sell every book you write, that the gig you did last year will be as lucrative when you return this year, that everything will be the way it was before (or better)? Is that realistic?

In short: of course not. In the real world, nothing is certain. Statistics can help you predict your success, but there are no guarantees. Having said that, though . . . you have to start somewhere, and historical data is a good place to begin. It's certainly better than making blind guesses in the dark. Accept that sometimes you're not going to make the expected sales, the trends will backfire in utterly unexpected ways or the plan you were planning on won't pan out. Make contingency plans and keep going!

As with everything relating to your art business, getting a handle on tracking and trending is going to take some time . . . but the results aren't just rewarding, they're necessary to your success.

What I Wish Someone Had Told Me When I Graduated College

Long, long ago, in the before-times, this Jaguar graduated from college with a Fine Art degree . . . in Studio Painting, with an almost-minor in Creative Writing. This degree prepared me for absolutely nothing useful (and in fact, did a poor job at the art stuff also, but that's a different story). I was poised at the edge of the Real World like a child at the edge of a pool, not entirely sure I wanted to dip my toes in. More importantly, I had no idea how to swim.

No one had told me anything about how to make it as a freelancer or a fine artist. Not the business principles I've spent several chapters discussing in this book, such as profit, revenue, expenses, tracking, marketing, etc. . . . nor even the most basic information like . . . how you even *set up* a business, legally.

These days, my alma mater teaches a class in just these fundamentals (entitled, sensibly enough, "Real World"). This chapter, though, is for those of you who graduated without the benefit of such a class: for those of you who, like young Jaguar, are staring out at the void and thinking, "Um . . . now what?"

Disclaimer 1: If you went to school to study for a specific job like copy-editor, animator, game-designer, etc . . . you don't need this chapter! Go forth and job-hunt, and good luck!

Disclaimer 2: There is no fourth Lawyer jaguar. This chapter does not constitute legal advice, which is why at the end of it I list actual places you can get legal advice. This is just a jaguar recounting (from her rather ratty notes) what it took to start a business here in Florida. And when I say "Florida," I really mean it. In other parts of the country, your procedure is going to be different. You will have to do the research.

Disclaimer 3: This chapter pertains to people living in America. I can't speak to other countries, except to guess— no, bet—that anywhere there's a government collecting taxes from people working, there will be paperwork and fees. Yours will just look different.

Paperwork

So, you want to get moving on this making money as a businessperson thing. Here are some of the steps—the ones I remember! They are that Byzantine.

1. If you plan to do business by anything other than your given name, you have to apply for a Fictitious Name. So, Baby Blue Parasols and Brightspirit Creations all have to be registered (which, of course, costs money). Then you have to run an ad in the newspaper for a couple of weeks notifying people of your intention to do business as that name. (Which also costs money.)

2. You will have to decide what kind of business you're running: a sole proprietorship, a partnership, a corporation (and there are now several types of corporation) . . . and all of them come with different requirements, laws, paperwork and fees. (And no, I can't tell you which is appropriate for you! You'll have to do the legwork and make the decision.)

3. You will need a license from the county (or parish, borough, etc.) to do business. And sometimes, from the city. If you're working from home, you have to make sure your county allows working from home, and if so if your business qualifies as one of the ones allowed (so they can prevent people from, say, slaughtering pigs next to other unsuspecting homeowners who might not like the reek). All

M.C.A. Hogarth

these things cost money. Plus, they have to be renewed. Mark your calendars.

4. You need to sign up for another license from your state's Revenue department, so they can collect sales taxes. For the state. You may also have to collect city or county sales taxes.

5. Depending on your company type, you may need to sign up for an employer tax ID number so the IRS can collect your earnings. For some reason, this service is free! Gee, I wonder why.

Fees and Taxes

Having gone through the rigmarole of legally setting yourself up, now you get to . . . pay more money! (I bet you thought I was going to say 'make money'. Ha!)

1. You will need to col- lect sales tax for your state (and/or city). De- pending on the size of your busi- ness, you'll be reporting sales tax between 1 and 4 times a year. If you're late send- ing it in, you will be fined. (I failed to

send mine in one quarter where I made no sales and got fined $50 for making no money. I now tape my slip to my wall in front of my face so I will remember.)

2. You will need to pay federal income tax. Also, there's a self-employment tax levied so that you can pay into Medicare, Social Security, etc. Don't expect a tax refund. Tax refunds are for parents and people who work for other people.

3. And, in some states, there's a state income tax. In case you thought some of the leftovers were yours.

But wait! There's more!

More Money You Need to Have

After you've given away your money to everyone who wanted it as a set-up fee, and then after you've given away your money to the people who want it quarterly, biannually or every year on a regular basis . . . you're still going to have to set apart money that you can't touch, because mark me, you're going to need it:

1. You will need to put money away in some kind of savings, because when emergencies come around, you'll be the one paying for them.

2. You will need to put money away for retirement, because no employer will be funding a 401(k) or pension plan for you. (You can set up your own 401(k), even. But you get to do the setting up.)

3. You will need to pay for health insurance. (Trust me. You will be paying for health insurance, no matter what the health care laws end up decreeing. The only difference is whether you'll be paying it out of your pocket or paying it at tax time.)

But What About Deductions?

Some of you may have heard that if you declare yourself as a business, you can handwave some of your bills. Contrary to nebulous rumor, a business doesn't get paid to buy stuff. Deductions allow you to detract the cost of something you use in your business . . . from the *profit* you made that year, for the purpose of reducing the amount you pay a tax on.

So if you make $500 a year, and would pay the IRS income tax on $500, but you spent $50 on supplies . . . then you pay the IRS taxes on . . . $450.

As you can see, this only puts money back in your pocket if you're making enough money to be taxed, and even then you can't reduce your tax burden past the amount you've made. If you make $500 a year and spend $1000, the government is not going to send *you* any money. Though wouldn't that be nice. :)

Don't take my word for It

I encourage you to investigate the legalities of doing business yourself. You will have to; my lists above are only guidelines based on hazy memories and should not be used as a checklist. Where you live will determine what hoops you'll have to jump through. Here are my suggestions for places to find all the information you need:

Business for the Right-Brained

- **Small Business Bureau.** Somewhere in your town the Small Business Bureau is running a Development Center to answer your questions about how to properly set up in your state. If you're serious about starting your freelancing business or just want to ask detailed questions, contact these people first.

- **An Accountant.** I encourage you to find a local accountant, preferably one who knows something about freelancing or art, and make an appointment to walk through the process of remitting all the money to all the proper places. The accountant will also be able to answer your questions about deductions, expenses and the fine print of your Profit & Loss. You'll need to have a working understanding of all these things, and the best person to give it to you is someone who does it day in, day out.

  You might never use this person's services again (and it can cost between $50 and $300 an hour depending on where you live), but this one appointment is important. Make it, take notes, get a business card in case you need help later.

- **IRS Website.** At some point you'll be swimming through the circulars on this site, so best bookmark it now.

- **An Artist's Group.** Preferably Local. Most towns will have one or more groups dedicated to working artists. Some of these groups will be useless, full of unherdable cats who can't even attend their own meetings . . . others will be an amazing investment, with seminars, classes, contests, forums and legal help. The only way to figure out which is to go have a look. I encourage you to stay local, or to at least find one local group in addition to any national ones, because local groups will be hooked into face-to-face opportunities and local grant/government/legal issues that you'll want or need to stay on top of.

- **Other Artists.** Similarly, maintaining a network of other artists at different points in their careers can help you keep track of problems to come and problems you haven't noticed yet. Someone selling at a fair in another state might warn you that you need to apply for a license there to report sales tax, for instance, or an artist more successful than you can tell you what provisions they've had to make when their volume hit a certain level. And it's always good to help people just starting, if you can: pay it forward.

- **The Library** . . . has an entire section devoted to running a business, from the very broad (running a business) to the very local (starting a business in your town) to the very specific (art marketing or freelancing opportunities). Go forth and browse! You're paying for it, after all.

The Legal Alternative to a Business

If all this sounds like too much trouble for the amount of money you're making, there are legal alternatives: for instance, you can declare your art a hobby, and list any income you make at tax time that way. As you might expect, reporting hobby income requires knowledge of . . . more tax law. For instance, declaring a profit for too many years may turn you into a business in the eyes of the government. Plus, you may be subject to self-employment taxes depending on how much profit you claim. And the laws governing deductions for hobbies are different from those for businesses. If you're making money at all, you'll have to become acquainted with the legalities . . . there's no getting around that. You can read more on hobbies and other ways of listing additional income at the IRS website, or you can make that accountant appointment to have someone walk you through the particulars.

Some of you will decide that you never want to go through the trouble of running your own business (or accepting any money at all!). There's nothing wrong with that. There are many days that *I* don't want the trouble. What the government calls your art-making activities for the purposes of taxing it have no bearing on what the art means to you or how seriously you take it. You can be skilled, passionate, talented and prolific and not accept a dime, so don't let the IRS's labels discourage you.

. . . So What I Wish Someone Had Told Me When I Graduated College:

Get a Day Job. (Find the right one, as per the Day Job chapter.) Use your spare time to hone your skills. Use your extra cash to buy reference materials and get extra tutoring, take classes if you can. Build a body of work. If you'd like to make money, then start selling your work and report your extra income. Learn about marketing and business basics. When your sales start looking very healthy—where 'healthy' means 'I can pay all those fees and bills and taxes and put away money for all that other stuff besides'—*then* you're ready to declare yourself as a business.

As with every other part of running a business, starting one is complicated and requires attention to detail. Don't jump in before you're sure of the waters . . . and yourself.

Enlisting the Aid of
Your Inner Customer

ONE OF THE MOST COMMON complaints I hear from people attempting their first business endeavor is "I'm no good at this marketing stuff!" I sympathize with this worry; marketing, as the customer-facing side of a business, is daunting. When we mess it up, we notice: sales are sluggish, clients are few or displeased and stress levels on both sides of the desk skyrocket.

I'm here to tell you, my friends, that inside you, right now! you have a personal trainer for your inner Marketer that will get her up to snuff in no time. She requires no work to find, no money to employ, and she's as merciless as a drill instructor.

The name of this hidden resource? *Your Inner Customer.*

Every day, you are the target of someone *else's* marketing attempts. Some days you buy. Some days you don't. Some days you are delighted and some days you rage. And every time some telemarketer calls you, a gangly teenager rings up your groceries or some friendly artist tries to sell you a piece of jewelry, your Inner Customer is awake and believe me, she's taking notes.

The Day I Made Formal Acquaintance with My Inner Customer

Long, long ago, I saw a piece of art in a convention art show that really spoke to me. At the time, being an impoverished college student, I couldn't afford the print. But I really, really liked it so I tried to figure out who the artist was and finally found her name by looking at the bid sheet attached to the piece I wanted.

Several years and a Real Job later, I shook out that note and went looking for her on Teh Intarwebz, and hooray! Found a website I could order from. I immediately bought that print and a week later, I received an envelope and tore into it.

. . . and out came the print.

Just the print, mind you. Not even wrapped in plastic. The corners of the piece were bent from bumps in transit, but luckily it had sustained no other damage.

Bewildered, I glanced inside the envelope . . . and found nothing else. No invoice or receipt, okay, fine . . . those are rare from individuals. But no business card? No pamphlet? No letter! I wanted *something* more from this transaction. I'd been anticipating buying this piece for years, and there was

Business for the Right-Brained

absolutely no ceremony to the consummation of my quest. Sitting there with the (slightly battered) print in my lap, I thought about what would have made me happy. A letter would have been amazing! Nothing personal, just a 'thanks for buying my print' form letter with a real signature, maybe. I would have been all over a business card or a pamphlet, or some piece of shiny paper that told me about what projects the artist was working on and what I might be interested in buying next. A catalog would probably have been too much to ask (though I would have eaten one up), but . . . I was really expecting more.

I still love that artist's work, and I can now afford her prices. But I haven't bought anything else from her. I don't *hate* her and I'm not angry about the product I bought from her. But she failed to connect with me when given a golden opportunity, and because of that I never think to spend my money on her work. I don't *remember* her when I splurge on artwork; instead, I spend my money on artists I interact with, or who I feel give something to their clients through blogging or similar online presences; or I turn to big companies like Allposters. com, from whom I do not expect personal interaction but who are timely and produce a high quality product.

The Rule

That day, with that sad envelope, I met my Inner Customer . . . and she passed on to me the one rule I use when planning any marketing endeavor. I am now passing that rule onto you, to see what your Inner Customer thinks of it. Like most rules of thumb, it's pretty simple. And here it is:

As a businessperson, do the stuff you wish
other businesspeople would do for you.

. . . that's it.

Applying the Rule

So how do you go about applying the rule? You have something you want to sell . . . imagine that you're someone who might be interested in buying. Ask these questions:

- How would I find out about This Thing? How do I *like* to find out about things like this? Do I hate receiving email? Do I notice ads? Is it reviews that move me? What if I'd really really like a thing, but no one's reviewed it yet . . . what would make me consider it anyway?

- What makes it convenient for me to buy Things like that? Do I prefer credit cards? Do I like sending money in the mail? Do I hate fussing with Paypal? Do I dislike working directly with people? Do I even really want to think about it? What would make it painless for me to part with my money?

- How do I like to be treated while considering whether I want to buy it? If I am treated courteously, would I recommend this merchant to someone else who likes this stuff, even if I decide I don't?

- How do I like to be treated while buying? What do I want the merchant to do for me? What kind of courtesies surprise and delight me?

Business for the Right-Brained

- How do I want to receive my product? Do I want it wrapped? Can it be damaged? Do I want customer letters? Care instructions? Do I want additional marketing materials? What would make me feel like the vendor either 1. cares about me personally, in the case of small businesses, or 2. looks like they know what they're doing, for big businesses?

All of which is very abstract, I know. Fortunately, imagining yourself as the recipient of your own services isn't the only way to employ your Inner Customer. You can also start recording how other people treat yours.

Negative Experiences

Whether or not negative experiences are more frequent, one thing's for certain: we sure do remember them better. So turn your blood-pressure-exploding moments into useful data by writing down *why* you were mad. Don't stop there, though! Write down two additional things:

- What would have prevented you from getting mad or upset? How could the business, the employee or the owner have changed things so that you would never have run into this problem?

- How could the business have appeased you after making the mistake?

So, for instance . . . that time the business shipped you the product and it showed up in multiple pieces. You were angry, of course . . . you paid for it and it's broken. You note they could have prevented the break from happening by packing it better—write that down, "always pack products carefully." But now that the thing is broke, what can they do to "make it right?" Negative customer experiences (Marketer Jaguar says) are always opportunities to go the extra mile to show a customer you care about their experience (because you do; it shouldn't be a lie). If you called the business and reported your broken product and they apologized and shipped you a new one, would that be enough to soothe your upset? What if they apologized and sent you a new one *and* a coupon? Would that change your feelings?

Case Study
I remember buying an art supply: a little bottle of masking fluid with an applicator. When I received it and attempted to use the applicator, it tore off. Perplexed (and disturbed, as it had not been a *cheap* art supply) I called the 1-800 number on the packaging, which was answered by . . . a real human being. Immediately. In fact, by the *owner*. A little startled, I

reported that the applicator had broken; with the distracted air of a mad genius, he asked me for the product code and proclaimed "That was my last model, I've improved the applicator since then. What's your address, I'll send you the new one!"

So I gave him the address and he mailed me an entirely new bottle, just like that. I have since discovered that I don't actually need that product . . . but whenever an artist says to me, "I need masking fluid," I bring out this long story, tell it enthusiastically and send him to the product's website. A negative experience was transformed by the business-owner into a positive one that now brings him advertising. That's what you want to aim for as a business-person . . . so pay attention when *you* are upset by a customer experience, and always take notes about how you could have been made to feel better about it . . . !

One final note on negative experiences: they don't have to be about anger. Disappointment or feelings of let-down are just as important, as in my example with the artist shipping me that print. Any time your Inner Customer's response to something is to sigh and say, "Oh well," or "ho-hum," bring out the questions! Why are you bored? What would excite you?

Positive Experiences

Yes, I know . . . it's quite rare to be delighted by your interactions with businesses. But it does happen. Sometimes it's just a faint relief, like "wow, that was easier than I expected." And sometimes, oh rare and wonderful sometimes, it's "OMG THAT WAS AWESOME."

Always take notes when something makes your Inner Customer happy. Sometimes it's quality. Sometimes it's competence. Sometimes it's the little things. But there are many ways to make a customer happy and you're not going to be able to think of all of them. Start building a file now on things that businesses have done that make you not only happy, but want to patronize them again and recommend them to others.

Case Studies

I use Clear Bags for my artwork. I remember vividly when I decided to start selling posters and realized I needed *something* I could ship rolled-up posters in. I browsed the Clear Bags website for half an hour, growing more and more distressed, until at last I picked up the phone and called them and rambled incoherently about what I needed.

The employee on the other end of the phone got me to measure my posters. He got me to measure the posters when they were rolled up. Then he set out three different options for me that he thought "might work," and then decided that wasn't good enough . . . he went back into his inventory stores, got out samples of each of the products he was recommending, and measured them on the spot to make sure they could take the diameter he had determined himself would be average for my posters. And there, on the phone, while I listened to him talking out loud, he finally said, "I think you really want this one, and this is why."

I said, instantly, "I'll take a roll of them."

That's how you make a customer happy.

Another example: when I had more free money, I sometimes used to buy custom clothing. On one occasion, I bought two similar pieces from two separate vendors. One of them arrived shoved into a manila envelope with an invoice. The other arrived in a box, wrapped in pink and purple tissue paper and ribbons, with business cards, care instructions, a signed letter and a pamphlet. It smelled faintly of roses.

Guess which vendor I still recommend? Actually, no, don't guess. Go check out Morua Designs.

Making a Habit of It

None of this will matter, of course, unless you make a habit of interviewing your Inner Customer. In fact, my recommendation is that you never really "turn her off." Whenever you're out buying things, being afflicted by marketing attempts or interacting with merchants, keep your Marketer present to have a dialogue with your Inner Customer. "Am I enjoying this? Am

I at least not upset about it? Was that good? Was that bad? Did I like how that employee treated me? Why?"

Don't stop at general observations; make a special point of observing other artists working in your field. What do they do that delights you? What do they do that annoys you?

I know one artist who writes a blog that is consistently fascinating, thoughtful and utterly focused on craft and art history. I buy his books. Interviewing my Inner Customer, I hear back: "I like people who share their knowledge and are friendly. And I like to think that the people I give money to are hard-working people who are constantly improving and researching their craft."

I know another artist who writes a blog that consistently links to politics that demonize half the population of the country. I don't buy his work. Interviewing my Inner Customer, I hear back: "It doesn't matter whether I agree with him or not. I don't like the lack of respect his attitude demonstrates for people he disagrees with."

The writer who keeps used copies of her out-of-print books to hand-sell to enthusiastic fans who can't find the book anywhere else: that's a great tactic, my Inner Customer thinks, and Far More Awesome than the writer who said, "I'm sorry, that's out of print," and nothing else. The costumer who does custom work, got messed up with health problems, and was honest, apologetic and up front about being behind schedule got my Inner Customer's admiration and sympathy rather than my irritation that she wasn't delivering. The artist who claimed she was poor and then later went on to talk about her shiny new purchases—I wasn't angry at her, but I didn't want to give her money anymore.

Business for the Right-Brained

This is the kind of information you should be collecting so you can become the kind of businessperson you'd buy from. Remember the rule: *As a businessperson, do the stuff you wish other businesspeople would do for you.*

THE INNER CUSTOMER IS NOT ALWAYS RIGHT

...BUT SHE'S STILL GOT THE MONEY.

Exceptions

No discussion about a person's Inner Customer would be complete without noting that for every rule there are exceptions. For instance . . . you might be the kind of person who wants to be left alone while making your decisions, while the person next to you wants a running commentary from a knowledgeable employee. You might not want small talk from your shopkeeper; you might find having to make personal connections with someone is just too much energy for you on a common day. A couple of notes, then:

- In some of the cases, you're not going to be as rare as you think. Try satisfying your customers the way you want to be satisfied and see if it works. In many cases, you'll find you'll attract people who'd like your work anyway. Like-minded artists often create work that attracts like-minded people—and shoppers.

- . . . if you tried the above and it *isn't* working . . . then you need to go observe other customers and see how they react to business-people to compensate for your quirk. This is an excuse to people-watch, which can be uncomfortable . . . but remember, you don't necessarily have to interview them. You just have to observe them.

Think of yourself as your first customer and design your business practices accordingly. You no less than anyone else have plenty of experience—and opinions!—on what makes a customer happy . . . so feed that data to your Inner Marketer and see what happens!

Time Management

INEVITABLY ANY MANUAL ON running your own business will edge toward a topic that that seems to prey on everyone's mind, a topic I avoided for a long time because so much has been written on it I had no idea what I could add. But then, inspiration struck! And so in this chapter, the three jaguars take on . . . time management!

Having read the chapters previous to this, you all might be expecting this topic to be a shoo-in for the inner Business Manager. In the past pages, I've talked about how Business Manager is in charge of budgeting, both money and time. In fact, most time management advice you find in magazines, blogs and books reads like dialogue straight out of inner Business Manager's mouth, with tips like:

1. Reclaiming lost time: how to comb your day looking for spare minutes and turn them into productive hours.

2. How to re-arrange your schedule to turn those spare minutes into bigger, more useful chunks of time.

3. How to find creative solutions to your time budgeting problems, like trading services with friends so you can work while they watch your kids, or you can cook while they find time to paint.

Which is all fine, fine advice . . . if you're already motivated to work. But let's face it. The problems most of us have with time management have nothing to do with process, technique or minutia. They have to do with attitude. With *desire*. And you know what that means.

It's time to say goodbye to Inner Business Manager:

. . . and say hello to the person in charge of the emotional aspects of your work life:

That's right. To really succeed at time management, the person you have to consult is your Inner Artist. Because the central tenet of time management is this simple: *If you really want it, you will find the time.*

Hey!

I know that right now a lot of you are bristling because (like me) you have been told over and over again that there's something wrong with you if you aren't willing to work hard at stuff you want. We place a high value on productivity in our culture, and we are absolutely tyrannical about punishing laziness. As a result, a lot of us frantically choose something, say to ourselves, 'this is it, this is what I'm going to be good at or interested in', and we spend years of our life bashing our heads in trying to accomplish it. The alternative (being seen as not doing anything at all) is worse than trying and not succeeding. Maybe along the way we convince ourselves that we really do

M.C.A. Hogarth

want what we're trying to do, or we invest so much time in it that we're afraid of back-pedaling and losing all those years.

But what applies to the Day Job applies to your creative life too. *There's nothing wrong with figuring out what you really want to do with your time and doing it.* Both on a macroscopic level—say, wanting to be a painter—and on the microscopic—like working on a particular project. And most time management problems begin at the microscopic level.

The Two Big Problems
In general, there are two problems that prevent us from making use of all those excellent Business Manager-like tips on time management.

"I'm . . . So . . . Bored With This!"
Maybe you were excited about it when you started. Or maybe you were never excited about it. Whichever applies, the fact is: the thing you're working on no longer inspires the Inner Artist, and when the Inner Artist gets bored she rarely reports in to work. You can try whipping her or bribing her, and sometimes that gets you somewhere. But art is about sharing something that moves you with the world. If a project no longer excites you, why are you torturing yourself finishing it? Choose something new and work on that instead.

Business for the Right-Brained

But wait! you say. Lots of things excite me, but once I start them, I lose interest! I want to finish *something!*

A good point! But while I'm a big fan of self-discipline, nothing greases the wheels like being interested in what you're doing. If you really want to finish that languishing project, here are some ways to find the passion again:

1. Re-read/look over your original notes for the project. Put yourself back in the headspace that conceived the idea. What excited you about it then? Is it still exciting? If not, is there a way to adjust the project to touch on themes or styles that are currently working for you?

2. Consider whether your approach to the project is the problem. Maybe you started a story as a novel, but it makes more sense as a short. Or the comic strip really needs to be a graphic novel. You wanted to do a steampunk costume but can't find the energy to finish it; do something radical with the rest of it, like changing it from a woman's dress to a man's coat tailored for a woman (or vice versa).

3. Go to your audience. Maybe you've forgotten all the reasons you wanted to finish something. But if you shared it with a friend, a critique group or some of your fans, they might be able to remind you. Tell them your interest is flagging and give them a chance to share *their* enthusiasm with you. Ask them to check in with you or ask you questions about it periodically.

Did any of these approaches work? If not, there's a second problem you might want to take a look at before you give up and move on:

"I'm Never . . . Ever . . . Going to Finish This. So Why Bother?"

An extremely common reason we lose interest in projects is the oppressive feeling that we will never complete them. If you can't see the end of the journey, it gets a lot harder to keep slogging on when the going gets tough (or boring). Whether we like it or not, we are wired to want the dopamine hit of accomplishment, and some projects are so tedious, long or difficult we feel we never get it. If looking at what you're working on makes you feel despair or apathy, or like you can't ever imagine what it will be like done, this is the problem you need to address.

1. First, if you've been tracking your average completion time on projects as I suggested in the Metrics chapter, drag those figures out now. Pluck out the figure that applies to the type of project you're working on now—say, 30 hours to finish a song—and post that figure somewhere. Figure

out how many hours you've logged on the project so far and tell yourself: "Hey . . . on average, I finish stuff like this in 30 hours, and I'm 10 hours into it. Another 20 to go!" Time yourself and keep going.

2. If you don't know how long your project usually takes—either because you haven't started time-tracking, or because you've never done anything like it before—don't despair. Have a look at where you want to end up: with a finished song or skirt or puppet or novel. Separate the project into discrete steps. "I need three verses, probably. A chorus. Two bridges." Or "I need to do the eyes, model the face, sew on the fur." Or "I need this character to end up here. I need a climax. I need some kind of ending." Once you do that, put up a "map" of your destination. Plan to reward yourself for reaching each discrete step.

3. Once again, appeal to an audience for help: a friend, a peer group, your fans. Not just to cheer you on; get them to tell you how far you've come. Their outsider's perspective might help reset your own, so you can see how far you've actually come instead of just how far you have to go.

Cutting Your Losses

You've tried to excite your Inner Artist. You've searched valiantly for the passion, you've cried on the shoulders of all your friends and fans, you've tried dangling carrots, making schedules, mapping imaginary destinations . . . and you still would rather play Farmville on your lunch break than work.

M.C.A. Hogarth

It may be time to move on.

But wait! Am I really saying you should give up?

Yes, I am—

—but giving up is bad!

. . . and it's not. Giving up is only bad if the goal you're abandoning is a worthwhile one for *you in particular* at this point in your life. The project you're failing to reinvigorate may not be the right project for you right now, and if it's not, you not only can give it up, you *need* to.

Why? Two reasons.

Your time is valuable. Let's be brutal in our candor. Most of us are doing this with what free time we have as it is. We work to put a roof over our heads. We come home, spend time with family, clean, cook, do more chores. The time we have left over has to be split between recreational activities that refresh us, our passions and sleep. If one of the activities you spend your spare time on is art, don't spend it doing something you aren't in love with. You owe it to yourself to work on the projects that excite you, which brings us to point number two:

Your passion is indispensible. If you wanted an activity that could be done on autopilot or through sheer willpower, you chose the wrong endeavor. Art is about passion. It's about working on things that excite you, that move you. It's about communicating that ferocity of spirit to your audience. Whether it's the stillness of a quiet joy, the pinpoint emptiness of sorrow, whether it's whimsy or joy or anger, whether it's your satisfaction at your own skills . . . the work is empty without *you* in it. Not all the technical mastery in the world will save a piece of art that has no soul. If you're doing this, your heart belongs in it. So don't waste your time on anything less.

This? This is your ticket to go. Notice that everyone is present to offer it to you. Business Manager knows how much time she'll lose trying to force you to work on something you don't care about. Marketer knows how hard it is to sell something that has no spark of life in it. And Artist . . . well, Artist wants to get busy on stuff that matters to her. Whether you need to let go of your dead project in steps and mourn it, or whether you can just take off and never look back, here is permission, if you need it.

But wait . . . !

The Money Problem

Ah yes. And here is the last of the problems. Some of you will have taken money to finish things you no longer care about . . . or never did. Now you're saddled with a project you have absolute zero interest in finishing. This is the point where a lot of art-business books will tell you how much you suck for not being a proper businessperson. (See above: re: our tyrannical need to punish laziness.) They will harangue you for not keeping to a schedule, for not being able to muster the discipline to power through something, or they will tell you to get the heck out of the business, because you're not cut out for it.

You can go read those books if you want recrimination. You're not going to find it here. The jaguars know that combining art with business is like navigating a swamp without a map during the rainy season. You don't know where you're going. You're not sure which parts are safe and which aren't. You think you're on solid ground until you try it, and then you discover: nope, you're sinking. There are no easy answers, and no one gets the right to smack someone else with a rolled-up newspaper as if there are.

So let's take care of the immediate problem: you have an assignment to do and you're having no luck with it.

1. Try changing your style/approach. If the parameters of your assignment allow you to play, you might be able to re-ignite your interest in it by doing it in some completely different way. You have to draw a book cover . . . instead of

the approach you were thinking of, try a completely different angle or style. You need to finish a short story for an
anthology . . . ditch your current idea and try a new plot.

2. . . . okay, you aren't allowed to change the parameters. You
    will have to slog through it, if you can. Try the incremen-
    tal goal technique I mentioned above; reward yourself for
    every 1000 words toward your goal, or for every step of
    the painting completed, or for writing one song toward the
    album. Be sure to stay in communication with your client,
    especially if you're getting close to the deadline (or par-
    ticularly!) if you've missed it.

3. Consider backing out, if you haven't spent the money al-
    ready. Give your client a full refund and your apologies.
    Don't be excessive or melodramatic; just tell them you've
    realized you're not a good fit for projects of this type.
    For extra profession-
    alism and customer
    care, identify several
    other artisans who can
    do similar work (and
    are professional in
    habit) and give
    their contact
    information to
    the client.

DO... NOT...
WANT!

So, having solved the immediate problem, you have some decisions to make. Was it this particular project that bored you? Or was it taking commissions in general? This is the difference between deciding that you don't ever want to do book covers for anyone, or you just don't want to do book covers that feature vampire lads ripping bodices off goth girls. You need this piece of information to decide whether you can accept money for this kind of work in the future. If it's being commissioned that you really don't enjoy, consider whether there's some other way to productize your work. (This goes back to my chapter earlier on uncovering what workstyle you enjoy.)

Running into a failure like this is valuable information, and inevitably you buy it dearly. Use it as an opportunity to further your understanding of your strengths and interests as a working artist. As I said above; your time is valuable and your passion indispensible. If you can save yourself upset in the future by admitting that you really just hate working to spec, or don't like a particular segment of the industry, or would rather just work on your own projects and figure out how to market them afterwards . . . then that's information you need in order to succeed on your own terms.

In Summary

Here's what I want you to take away from this chapter:

1. Time management starts with your inner Artist. If she's not interested, not all the tips and tricks in the world will help you.

2. Unless you have a pressing need otherwise, you owe it to yourself to work on things that excite you.

3. If you can't finish something, it doesn't make you lazy, stupid or useless. It just means what you were working on wasn't the right thing for you, right now.

4. If you want to make money at art, it helps to find a product that you enjoy making; taking money to do things you despise will not lead you to a productive, fulfilling working life.

There are exceptions to this, of course. But in general, time management is as much a matter of passion as it is about discipline. If you spend most of your time forcing yourself to work or finding reasons not to, then you're not heeding the call of your inner Artist. That's a much bigger problem than whether you can shave ten minutes off your commute so you can spend that time writing.

Un-Slimy Marketing

I T WAS OUR PLAN TO DEVOTE a chapter to the value of self-discipline . . . but that was before you spoke and nearly over-whelmingly asked how to market yourself without feeling slimy. Naturally, this woke the Marketer Jaguar, whose first response was something like this:

And then she went to work, because we're here to answer your questions and this one's obviously burning at your minds. So, let's talk about how to feel good marketing yourself, and make friends doing it. It can be done!

Now, we all know marketing we like. And we all know marketing we don't. Our problem then, is figuring out what separates the "okay" marketing from the "hate them never want to hear from them again disgusting used-car-salesman ick" marketing so we can stay on the good side of the equation. As far as Marketer Jaguar is concerned, there are three stages of marketing technique, rising from the dregs of slime to the rarified clouds of awesome customer relationships.

STAGE ONE MARKETING IS
NOT VERY SUBTLE.

Business for the Right-Brained

Stage One: Gimme Your Money

In the first stage of marketing, your goal is to get people to give you their money. You spend a lot of time thinking about getting money out of people. Or about finding more people to get money out of. You strive very hard to remain upbeat about selling your art, but you probably have thoughts like these:

1. That other artist just sold something! I'm jealous!

2. That's one of my fans, talking about buying something. I wish they'd spend that money on me.

3. Nobody's buying my work. Why won't they buy my work, when crap like [Highly Successful Artist, like Thomas Kincaide] sells like hotcakes?

Stage One Marketing results in marketing tactics like these:

1. Being reluctant to link to other artists' work because people might spend their money on them instead of on you.

2. Talking about your bills or problems to help people justify spending money on your work.

3. Rarely talking about anything but money or sales.

If you are fixated on money, your audience will notice. They won't like it. And if you ever make the mistake of voicing those thoughts up there where other people can see them, you will have a lot of public relations work to do to repair your image. It's hard not to linger in this mindset when so many of us are desperate to pay bills, or to get some sense of validation in a society that only seems to recognize the ability to earn money as an indicator of value. But if you want to be content as a creative professional, you need to move up the ladder. Let's consider stage two.

STAGE TWO IS ALL ABOUT YOU, BABY!

Stage Two: I'm Excited About My Stuff!

At stage two, your enthusiasm for your work bubbleth over, and you are effusive about sharing that enthusiasm with everyone. You love your new projects; you talk about them all the time. This is one of the few places where the Artist drives the marketing effort, because she just can't. Not. TALK ABOUT THE AWESOME! You regularly inhabit stage two if your communication with the outside world is stuff like this:

1. The chapter I just wrote, it just FLOWED out of my fingers! I can't wait to post it!

2. My new brushes just shipped! I haven't used a new brush in months, it makes finicky detail-work so much better!

3. My new album is coming out next week, and I just love this one, it's my best ever!

Stage Two Marketing results in marketing efforts like these:

1. Spending a lot of time talking to, hanging out with or writing blog posts that appeal to other artists in your field.

2. Offering sneak peeks of things you're currently working on.

3. Talking about what you're working on now, even if you can't share it yet.

Now, to be honest, if you were to stop here at this stage, you'd probably be fine. Most people forgive artists some amount of narcissism. Bubbling about your work will incite excitement from your current fans and net you some new ones, and some people get by fine with that. However, you will drive away some number of people who will find your self-satisfaction excessive and your constant talk about things they can (or can't yet!) buy frustrating. And this inward focus prevents you from rising to the third marketing stage, where Artist looks outside herself and notices . . .

STAGE THREE IS ALL ABOUT THE
CONNECTION.

Stage Three: My Work Lets Me Develop
Relationships with Cool People

. . . other people. This is the point where you look beyond your desk and really feel in your bones that art is communicative: it speaks to the people who like it, and that means the two of you have something in common. And you find you are delighted at the opportunity to meet these people. You're at this point when you often think or say things like this:

1. I love doing readings because at the end I get to talk to my fans!

2. I know her; she bought several big ticket items from me before. I think I'll send her a card for the holidays.

3. I am grateful for my fans and patrons. So many awesome people like my work!

Stage Three Marketing results in efforts like these:

1. Writing ad copy while imagining you're talking to some-one. Maybe even someone specific.

2. Setting up kaffeeklatsches at the next convention so you have time to talk with your fans.

3. Giving free advice to people who want to want to follow a path similar to yours.

Notice that by this point, you come full circle: in stage one, you are bitter because people aren't giving you money. By stage three, you're delighted because people give you money.

But wait! You say. Do I have to take these stages one by one?

Of course not! I talk about the stages as if we could move through them sequentially, but most of us will bounce between them depending on the day, the art in front of us, and our mood. Our goal, though, is to head away from an attitude that breeds resentment, discontent and negativity and toward one that enhances our relationships with each other and our art.

Why?

Because marketing is about our relationships with other people.

Yes . . . I'm serious! Just because the connection created by marketing is fleeting doesn't make it meaningless. The cashier who smiles at you, meets your eyes and chats with you while ringing up your groceries is sustaining, for that brief moment, a relationship with you. You leave a store feeling more positive, neutral or negative depending on the interaction you've had with the people selling you things. And as an artist in particular, your relationship with your audience is more intimate because of the nature of your product. You are selling the work of your hands and heart, and that makes any transaction between you and someone interacting with it implicitly a deeper thing.

The people who love and buy your work have something in common with you, and that thing is something that came from in your heart. That makes them kin to you, if only in passing. If you hold that knowledge in your heart when selling your work—that you are not seeking money so much as seeking kin—then chances are you'll be far happier with your business (no matter how small) than if you're in it for the money . . . which, I must tell you frankly, is a rather bad focus for an endeavor like art-making. There are easier and surer ways to make a buck.

The Jaguar's Philosophy of Marketing

Here then, in brief, is what I believe: that your goal in marketing is to create sustainable relationships with people who want you to succeed; in short, to seek patrons, rather than one-time customers. To do that, you can't be focused on the money or the one-time sale. You want to inspire customer loyalty. You want people to be invested in your success. You want them to feel special . . . because they are. We live in a society where marketing treats its customers as prey . . . or victims, happy to pluck their last dollar out of their pocket while convincing them that what they're getting is what they really need, whether that's true or not. Such a system isn't sustainable; eventually, people will run out of money while surrounded in unnecessary stuff, and they will have no money to succeed themselves. The whole thing will grind to a slow, ugly halt.

You know you don't want to be a part of that system; you wouldn't have told me overwhelmingly that marketing feels slimy to you otherwise. So take the jaguar's advice. Think of your customers as people and your marketing efforts as an attempt to *make it easy for people who want your work to buy it,* not an attempt to get more people to buy your work, whether they would have chosen to or not. If you're not happy with how much money is coming in, then your next big step is not marketing—getting interested people to buy—but *advertising,* which is the art of reaching more people in the hopes of locating your next patrons.

But that's a whole other topic. Frankly, that might be a whole other book.

In Review . . .

If your twitter stream contains statements like these:

*I feel like I'll never make it . . . why
can't I seem to sell enough?*

. . . you are in stage one. Save your bitterness and doubt for your confidants and move on.

If your twitter stream contains mostly statements like these:

*This next album is going to be
awesome! It's writing itself!*

. . . you are in stage two, and are entertaining people who are already your fans while occasionally putting off people who aren't. If this is what you can manage most days, you're in good shape.

If your twitter stream contains stuff like this:

*Good morning! How are you all today? You've been
asking me for more stories about CharacterName,
so I'm working on a story about him right now!*

. . . then you've successfully moved the focus to a balance between yourself and others, and you're doing great. Keep it up!

Remember: we are all custodians of our economic

ecosystem, and that means both spending our money wise-ly . . . and selling our art in a way that respects our patrons' humanity. If you keep your focus in the right space—the one between you and your customer—you'll find it much easier to avoid the pitfalls of the used-car-salesman approach to marketing.

Agility

T HIS CHAPTER IS ON ONE of our favorite things: Change.

The Jaguar and the Database

Long, long ago, in the before times, your humble author was working in a software development shop when yet another take on the eternal push to make coding faster and more responsive to customer demands was published, this one entitled the Agile Manifesto (you can read more about that on-line by searching for it, if you're interested in the tangent). The powers that be decided to adopt this methodology out of a gut understanding that to be agile in business is a good thing. I didn't perceive the adoption of the Agile Methodology to do anything more than confuse the coding department, but the concept stuck with me.

It's with me even now, while I look at the wreck of my customer database. Because I have a customer database.

But Jaguar! (you say). Why is this strange?

Because I have a customer database . . . as a writer. And I have no templates for how an author uses a customer database because traditionally the work of connecting with customers was undertaken by retailers, who distributed a book sent to them by someone (a distributor) that was supplied by someone (a publisher) who connected with me through someone else (an agent). That's a lot of layers between me and the people who would have bought my books, and therefore between me and the necessity of having a spreadsheet with people's names and purchasing histories. Had I been through the traditional publishing process, I wouldn't have needed a customer database. In fact, it would have been rare for me to know the people who bought my books at all unless I met them at a pre-arranged event like a convention or a book signing. But thanks to the wonder of technology and the society it's changing, I can and do sell my work directly to readers. I post my work online, someone passes me a tip . . . and now I know a name. When I learn a customer name, I write it down (or should).

The paradigm has changed. Simple, right?

It's Never Simple!

Except . . . that I don't just sell directly to readers. I also sell my work through distributors, who distribute it to people who have bought it. I don't know the names of those customers (unless they contact me, or leave a review with their names on it). And instead of taking money directly from those people, I am now policing one (or several!) distributors who owe me royalty checks.

So now I have a customer database which is incomplete, causing my inner Business Manager much upset over the lack of tidiness and my inner Marketer much melancholy over lost opportunities. And I have more than one way of earning money, all of which have to be tracked, maintained and audited. And if I choose to sell in other ways, I'll only end up compounding the complication of my business tracking procedures. Mostly I find myself thinking that this is a lot of work, and that had things remained the way they were before, I wouldn't have incurred that work at all. Someone else would be tracking customers, leaving me more time to write.

And here is where I return again to the concept of agility, and the fact that necessitates it: Business changes. Society changes. Technology changes. The bad news is that if you aren't able to move with those changes, you're not going to make it. The good news? If you are creative about seizing those opportunities, you may waste some time here and there, but you have a chance not just to make it, but to make it big. Or at very least, big by an artist's standards, which means you'll be comfortable and able to do your thing in peace. More or less!

Let's Get Concrete

So, how to stay agile in the art business?

1. First, and most importantly: develop the mindset that changes do not affect you; you take advantage of changes. (You see how "you" became the actor in that second sentence, rather than the object being acted upon?) Changes are opportunities. Think of changes as ways to break out of ruts, find new revenue streams or expand your customer base. You are not the victim of change. You are one of its users. When change comes along, start thinking of ways to make it work for you, rather than bemoaning the loss of whatever it's trampled.

2. You can't use a change you don't know about. Keep abreast of developments in your field: magazines and paper newspapers can often be late with their news, so use twitter, blogs and online resources when you can. The sooner you know about changes, the more time you have to think about how you can use them to your advantage.

3. Related to #2, identify the industry leaders in your arena and keep an eye on them. Some companies are consistent

innovators, whether it's tech-
nologically or process-wise.
Where they go, often
the market follows.

4. Always budget
   some amount of
   money for tech-
   nology up-
   grades and mar-
   ket research. Is the
   hottest new thing
   in your target market a
   tablet? Save up and get one. Is there some new program
   that is all the rage among digital artists? Ditto. Whether
   it's new shopping cart code or a new kind of brush, learning about something game-changing is not usually enough
   for you to really understand its possibilities. Get one and
   play with it and things will occur to you that never will if it
   remains a thought exercise. If your budget is too small to
   buy, find someone willing to lend their shiny to you, or go
   to a store and play with the floor model.

5. Never get too attached to your processes. We all like a
   routine and we all want to stick with what works, but if
   you never experiment you might miss out on your Next
   Big Thing. If this idea makes you uncomfortable, remind
   yourself that you don't have to stick with it if it's not working for you. And remember: you are not your tools or your
   processes, which exist only to facilitate your work. If the

process or the tools no longer serve the art, or no longer serve it well enough, discard them. The art will remain. It is above and beyond those things.

6. Keep in mind that even if something is working for you now, changes might make it impossible to continue making money that way. It doesn't matter how good a buggy whip you make when the first car rolls off the assembly line.

7. Listen to what your customers/patrons want. They will tell you what they're willing to pay for before you've thought of it, or are ready for it! When someone who buys your work says, "I wish—" that's your cue to listen very carefully to what comes next. Make sure your knee-jerk reaction to those comments is not "I don't do that." Train yourself to say, "I'll look into that," or "That's a very interesting idea, I can't do it now but I'll do some research into it," or "I'm not set up for that—yet!" And believe it when you say it. And then do it.

8. Finally, be okay with mess. Change is rarely simple and never complete. Selling e-books doesn't mean I can't sell through publishers doesn't mean I can't sell a serial doesn't mean . . . etc, etc. If you can't find rules, processes or anything more concrete than suggestions for how to handle the things you're trying, that's a sign that you're on the track of something new and exciting. Congratulations, put on your hat. You're a pioneer!

Art, which is often shared or sold via some form of media, is very vulnerable to the technological and social advances that are common today. If you want to make art, none of it need concern you . . . but if you want to make money from art, then you have to pay close attention to the way people transmit and consume content. That makes it a very exciting time to be working, and a very tumultuous one! Keeping the above points in mind may help you keep your head above water . . . and maybe even seize some opportunities of your own.

Pricing (or, the 99 Cent E-Book)

NINETY-NINE CENT E-BOOKS! Who would have thought we'd ever see the day! And yet, if you check your online retailer, there they are! This price is very intriguing to the Jaguars . . .

. . . well, to two of the Jaguars.

That's right. Business Manager and Marketer are perfectly

fine with this notion, but Artist is not. And the heart of this disagreement is pricing, a topic so large that when the three jaguars began discussing it, it ballooned into an enormous discussion with lots of pictures!

We have a lot to cover! So let's begin . . . with philosophy!

The Disgruntled Artist

It should come as no surprise that in a society that so tightly (and capriciously) links money with worth, Artist might be distressed that her work might end up costing the same amount as a gumball from a candy machine. And yet, if Artist were to attempt to get some picture of what something is worth by its price, look at the mixed signals she would get:

What can you take away from the realization that a piece of cake in a restaurant can cost more than a pack of light bulbs? Or that a piece of underwear can cost the same amount as a cup of coffee? Nothing about the absolute worth of underwear or coffee. Pricing makes even less sense when applied to art. Who could ever figure out what it's worth to them, a song that they've loved for years, a book that changed their lives? One dollar? A million? Art is irreplaceable in the hearts of those it touches. But the products you make based on your art, those have a definitive monetary value within the market ecosystem, and your job as a businessperson is to find that price point.

Pricing and money apply to *products*, and it is only as products that we can assign prices and judge their suitability.

This is why coffee can cost more than underwear, and cake more than light bulbs: because they are productized differently. Light bulbs and underwear are far more useful, more necessary, than cake and coffee, but what you pay for is the presentation, packaging and marketing experience on the latter two items, not their intrinsic worth.

Let us put paid to the myth then: artistic merit and money are not equivalent. When you approach the question of pricing, you must set aside passion (the Artist's driving attribute) and turn instead to issues of setting buyer expectations, deciding which markets to compete in and gating customer demand. Pricing is the realm of Marketer and Business Manager, so send Artist back to her easel.

So then, let's begin with the example above: the 99-cent e-book. This may seem a gross devaluation of work to Artist, who appears here as understandably skeptical. Here are her thoughts:

- Books are not songs, and should not be priced like them. Art forms are not interchangeable!

- How will people know that it's worthwhile if it's only 99 cents?

- If enough authors price their work at 99 cents, people will stop paying for $10 books, and then how will authors make a living?

- Other people's books are priced at $10 or even $15, so why should Artist's be any less? It will make her look cheap!

- She's spent months of her life on the story. Shouldn't she be compensated?

Books Are Not Songs! Or, Competition

Let's begin with Artist's first objection: that just because other forms of art are priced a certain way, that every form of art should be. There is a poorly-grasped marketing truth here, which we will clarify now:

Different forms of art are priced differently
because they are productized differently.

A song and a story are both priceless things that float apart from monetary value. But a download of an MP3 and a DRM-free e-book are both *products* and have a market value which may (or may not!) be distinct from one another.

So to get our hands around the concept of a song costing the same thing as a book, we have to separate the art itself from the product. No, music, dance, art, writing . . . on a superficial level, these are not the same things. But if they are productized, distributed and marketed in similar ways, then we run into the great leveler:

Competition.

. . . because a book may not be like a song. And a song might not be like a photo online. And it may not be like a game or an app. But all these things are the same to your buyer: *they are all luxury items consumed as entertainment.* And that means they're all competing against one another for the person's time and money. Say your fan has $10 to spend a month on entertainment. He can use that money on books, movies, music, games, World of Warcraft subscriptions, tickets to sporting events . . . whatever floats his boat. Your job as a business-person is to make it easier for him to choose your stuff instead of someone else's.

Step back a moment and truly consider this: The work of your life and hands and spirit, once it hits the marketplace, is sold just like any other commodity. And while we don't want to think of ourselves as interchangeable with other artists—and our fans might assure us that we aren't—our products are not the only products our fans are interested in. Inevitably, they (not being possessed of infinite wealth or time) will have to choose. And while there are customers who cleave only to one form of art, forsaking all others—a person who only likes to read and is bored by music, dance, visual art, games, etc—these people are rare and one should not rely on them for one's livelihood.

In Conclusion

All Artist's beliefs about the singularity of whatever art form she practices aside, her work, once it reaches the market, must be able to compete in price and value with art, games and entertainment of every other kind. It doesn't matter if an app isn't like a song, and a song isn't like a piece of art. It's a discretionary purchase, and your customer has to perceive that it's not just a good value for his money, but a better one than something else. If ten songs can be bought for the price of one of your books, then your book has a lot more work to do to convince someone to buy it instead of ten songs. Or five songs and an app. Or one poem, three songs and two cows in a farming game.

Does it outrage the poor Artist? Indubitably. But it remains an economic reality.

How Will People Know It's Good if It's Only 99 cents? Or, Identifying Real Worth

Artist's next objection is a good one: price does drive perception of worth. But what she misses is that it doesn't drive the perception of the worth of the *art*, but rather the worth of the *product*. $15 for a life-changing book is as nonsensical as 15 cents. But $15 for a physical object makes sense because it possesses qualities the market perceives as more valuable.

Art, as we have discussed before, cannot be sold. It must be productized. If your goal is to make a living, you should be brainstorming and releasing products that have as many market-valuable characteristics as you can manage. Different audiences will have different ideas of what's valuable, but among the set of people who buy art, here are some common characteristics:

• **Physicality.** Many forms of art can be delivered digitally—as an e-book, a copy of a jpeg, a download, etc. If it can be packaged as an object, people tend to value it more, particularly if they have the choice between physical and digital versions. A physical book, a pressed CD, a print . . . all these things can be sold for more money because most people like to touch things with their hands.

- **Immediacy.** Some forms of art are initially delivered as performances, such as music, dance, theater, and people are willing to pay more in order to have the immediate experience of the art, more than they would for a recording. With some creativity, unlikely art forms can also be productized this way: art can be created in person or on camera (the popular "Iron Artist" contests at conventions come to mind), stories can be livewritten with prompts from the audience, jewelry can be fashioned to spec in person, etc.

- **Uniqueness.** One of the great prizes of marketing is uniqueness, because people will pay large sums of money for something for which there is no copy, or which there are poor copies. The actual canvas an artist has touched is worth more than a reproduction. Hand-crocheted hats are worth more than machine-made. The original manuscripts for famous books are auctioned and put in museum collections. We value ties to individual people, and

unique items are irreplaceable for their ability to connect us with an artist.

- **Portability.** As we move further into a digital market, consumers value access to different versions of a piece of art. A physical book with included digital copy is worth more than either alone. A DRM-free song is worth more than a locked one.

- **Ownership.** As the digital market splinters into pay-to-access and pay-to-own spheres, consumers will always privilege ownership over access rights. People enjoy the idea that buying something entitles them to dispose of it as they choose, and remain concerned that paying for access will deprive them of the art in the future if technology or circumstances change.

- **Personalization.** Because most people value a connection between themselves and the artists they patronize, any form of personalization is good. This is the need that drives people to stand in line for book signings, or bid on signed baseballs, to commission art or have their names written into songs. Most forms of art can be personalized either during the creation process (as in commissions and prompts) or after (signing, added packaging, etc). A print is worth a certain amount of money. A print that a client is able to have matted in the color that matches her living room is worth more.

- **Personal Attention.** Closely related to personalization is personal attention, the sense that one can have a dialogue with and even some kind of relationship with the artist in question. People value the ability to shake a hand and look in someone's eye. They like to be remembered as the customer who likes dragons or the client who needs her items mailed to her workplace rather than to her house. Any time you are responsive, communicative and able to accommodate special requests, you are delivering personal attention.

A good gut-instinct guideline for determining premium services: the more senses a product engages, the more money you can ask for it. If you can touch and hear something as well as see it, you're better off than if you can only see it. An original piece of artwork even has a smell depending on what it was made with. Sensory input makes things real to people; studies show that people who can touch products are more likely to buy them. So go with your gut and make your products as sensuous an experience as possible.

Many of the characteristics above can be combined. The more of them you stack in a single product, the more money you can ask for, and should. A DRM-locked e-book of a 300-page novel may only be worth four bucks. The same novel, as a special edition with a foil-embossed cover, signed and dedicated to a specific customer by the author and annotated in the margins with notes, presented in person with a "thank you for buying" card, may be worth several hundred.

How Will I Make a Living if Everyone's Pricing Their Stuff So Cheap? Or, Market Awareness

In a market where every product of a similar type is priced along similar lines, the one product that's more expensive had better have a good reason for its exemption or no one will take it home . . . and the one product that's less expensive will, if it's perceived to be of similar quality, be the sales leader. When artists rally around one another and decide, en masse, to keep their prices at a certain level, they are attempting to protect themselves from those devaluations.

. . . and it doesn't work. Inevitably, someone will decide to sell for cheaper in order to sell more often or in greater volume, and then the whole scheme collapses.

As an artist selling products based on your work, you have two jobs, then:

1. Research the current market value for the product you're attempting to sell, and figure out how to make it cheaper;

2. And guess how the market is going to change to make that price invalid.

You can imagine neither of these activities is low-stress. They are both, however, necessary. You are competing in a market that is vulnerable to technological change, and nothing affects pricing like technology.

Your goal, as much as possible, is to liberate your particular product from the price fluctuations of the market. You can do this by attempting to create a price monopoly, as in the (poorly orchestrated) attempt I once witnessed wherein furry artists tried to set baseline prices for services they sold at conventions (this price monopoly lasted *maybe* a month). Or you can be more successful at it by constantly seeking ways to make your product cheaper to produce.

The rule is very simple:

STEP 1: MAXIMIZE REVENUE

STEP 2: MINIMIZE EXPENSES

STEP 3: PROFIT

(THERE IS NO MISSING STEP.)

Case Study: Art Cards

For instance. You draw 3"x5" art cards to spec, an activity that takes you an hour per piece. In the current market atmosphere, artists sell these for between $15 and $30. You price them at $20. It costs you $6 in materials and time to create these cards, so a price of $20 allows you to make $14 an hour after expenses.

You can continue to price these at $20 and hope the market allows that price to remain reasonable. Or you can attempt to maximize your profit level by trying these things to mini-mize your expenses:

1. Learning to execute the art more quickly, either by chang-ing style or detail level, or practicing until you get faster, so that you can do more pieces per hour.

2. Buying your supplies in bulk or on sale to push down the material cost per piece.

3. Deciding to sell these card commissions as phone or tablet backgrounds, doing away with physical costs completely. Or these things to maximize your revenue:

1. Selling prints of the resulting art cards.

2. Finding a market niche that supports a higher per-piece level—for example, marketing to people who like pictures of reptiles and can't find many.

3. Selling the digital rights separately from the physical prod-uct, and offering both to the customer.

Say the floor falls out from under your $20 price and you find yourself forced to reduce your prices to $10 in order to secure more commissions. If it takes you $6 to create the card, you are now only making $4 a card! But if you cut your ex-penses in half, you're up to $7. And if you add extra revenue-generating activities, you might double your returns.

The point? "How will I make a living?" is a question that

can only be answered by constant assessment of the market, and constant adjustment of your product strategy. If your publisher sells your e-books for $15 each because every other publisher does, then you're in good shape . . . until the first independent author comes along and undercuts you by $10. If your books stop selling well, your choice is to take the hit or find a way to make money in some other way to supplement your income. You cannot depend on the way it's been done before to save you, which brings us to . . .

Other People's Books Are Priced at $15!
Or, Pricing and (Lack of) Precedence

We've said before that art is often productized, delivered and marketed in a way that makes it particularly vulnerable to technological change. If there is a truth to be embraced about pricing—about business in general—it's right here:

How it was done before doesn't matter. How it's done *now* doesn't matter. To really succeed, you need to be guessing how it's going to be done tomorrow . . . and doing it.

People's expectations are changing with the technology, not with the art form. With smartphones widespread, people's expectations will be shaped by 99 cent apps and $2 games. With tablets more broadly accepted, people's expectations will be shaped by digital magazines, downloadable wallpapers and artists offering commissions on graphic apps. With e-book readers everywhere, people's expectations are shaped by the instant gratification of the immediate download . . . and the low-tech format of their e-book.

Everywhere around you, technology is shaping what people expect, how they consume art and what they expect to pay for it. Their beliefs will be shaped not by the worth of the art, but by the characteristics of the product. Do they own it? Can they reproduce it? Is it high or low-resolution? Is it personal? Is it immediate?

It doesn't matter how art is priced now. What matters is how it's packaged and how much people perceive that packaging to be worth. You can't afford to get attached to how much someone else is selling something for. Chances are good that tomorrow, people will have moved on to something else they believe gives them better value for their dollar.

Case Study: or, the 99 Cent E-book

An excellent case in point: the discussion that inspired this chapter involved the three—well, two—jaguars proclaiming they were all in favor of 99 cent e-books. At no point in the ensuing dialogue did anyone bring up the very important distinction that the three jaguars were talking about . . . e-books.

E-books. Not *novels*.

The existing industry standards developed while productizing and marketing stories issued on paper. As such, length was key. Long books cost more to produce: they had a higher physical material cost (more paper, glue, etc) and they took up more space in inventory. But very short works were just as difficult to issue in paper: their length made producing them as single items cost-ineffective, and attempts to productize them using the same method as long-form works—producing things that looked like novels but contained short stories—rarely inspired the sales volume necessary to recoup the investment.

In addition, length dictated much of the editorial guidelines as editors strove to find a bal-ance between the stories they wanted to publish and the limitations of their paper vehicles. Authors couldn't sell novellas because they took up too much space in short fiction markets and not enough in novel markets. Books ended up split into parts that were never intended to be sold that way because of their size as physical volumes (see: *The Lord of the Rings*).

SAME STORY...

...NOT THE SAME PRODUCT!

But whether an e-book is one page or one thousand, it is still sold through the same channels and is packaged, on the surface, in the same way. Browsing the average e-bookstore, most consumers won't even realize how long the story they're buying is. We don't speak of e-novels and e-novellas and e-short stories, but of e-books. And as such, 99 cents is a perfect price point for an e-book . . . which is short in length.

Why? Because where there is no obvious indicator of length, price is a great vehicle for communicating this information to the buyer.

Books have not been sold in this fashion before. Most hardcovers are $25 (right now). Most trade paperbacks are $15 (right now). Most paperbacks are $8.99 (right now). If a book isn't long enough to look good as a $25 hardcover, layout artists will arrange the text until it takes up the right amount of pages. (This is why sometimes you buy a hardcover and it seems more whitespace than text.) Books don't need to price for length, since they can make any book's spine look about the same as another's with tricks like font size and leading. Instead, the implication of the existing pricing tier is that you are paying for longevity/sturdiness: $25 for a hardcover that you can keep for decades and $9 for a paperback that will probably fall apart in a year, with trade paperbacks a compromise between the two.

But we are in a new market now, with new needs. Consumers are already used to thinking of price as an indicator of volume: you pay $5 for a small bottle of honey and $15 for two pounds, and of course, two pounds is more than the little bottle. Translating that thinking to e-books works fairly well. Paying 99 cents for a short story and $4 for a novel? One is longer than the other. Of course! But because we become trapped in How Things Were Before, we often don't even see how the *product* a piece of art becomes can change so radically with technology as to need entirely new pricing . . . and terminology.

E-book. Novel. Not equivalent. You can't apply paper standards to electronic packaging.

I've Spent Months of My Life on This! Or Gating

Artist has a vague sense that she deserves to be compensated for the time she spends making art. Even more than that, she perceives that the life experience she alchemizes into art has value, that she deserves as least as much an hour as some database programmer somewhere. But in general, Artist's conception of these things is nebulous.

To really talk about this objection, we need the Business Manager.

If you've read the previous chapters, you'll recall that time-tracking—logging the hours it takes to produce a single piece of art—is one of Business Manager's jobs. Her goal in doing so is to give those statistics to Marketer with the injunction, "Make this worth my time."

Marketer says, "Okay!" and goes to work. Her job: to take this single piece of art and make as many products from it as possible, pricing them at what the market will bear, in order to recoup the time and material cost of the project and make a profit.

Business for the Right-Brained

Scenario 1: Too Much Time

So, say, you need a year to write a novel. Artist delivers it. Business Manager frowns at the time, then tells Marketer, "Twelve months, one piece of art. Have at it."

. . . and now Marketer has the unenviable task of trying to make a year's worth of income from a single piece of art.

She might try any number of tactics: cheap e-books, sold in volume. Physical copies, also sold in volume. Premium special editions for high-end collectors. Merchandise, such as mugs with taglines from the novel or shirts with the cover art. Auctions of scribbled notes made during the art process, unique items representing glimpses into the writer-brain. She might try advertising, cross-pollination with other artists, book signings and appearances. And if she's lucky as well as exceptional, she might turn one piece of art into a year's income. Might.

It's tempting to make everything more expensive so that she'll get a better profit per item . . . but raising prices makes sales sluggish, particularly if they're above the market average. That is not a good solution. What's far more likely is that she'll return to Artist and Business Manager and say, "Make more art faster."

Sad fact: with rare exception, a single masterpiece every few years will not suffice to earn your bread. If you work slowly and don't want to work any faster, or don't believe you can, then you must content yourself with a very small salary. If you want better income, you will have to learn to either become a genius at marketing—not a task to which most artists want to apply themselves—or figure out how to produce art more frequently.

Scenario two: Too Little Time

On the other hand, maybe you write a short story every week, a novel every two months and fill in all the extra spaces with essays, poems and columns. Artist enters the studio every day and exits it in a burst of fluttering papers. Business Manager looks at this blankly, then hands a ginormous stack of things to Marketer and says, "Um, enjoy!"

Marketer looks at it all and has a momentary spasm of joy. And then slowly, a louring sense of doom. She knows:

1. Placing this much work takes time. If it takes three hours to completely productize one piece of art, imagine the administrative time involved doing sixty.

Business for the Right-Brained

2. Placing too much work on the market at a time can flood it, particularly if you are operating in a single arena. If Artist is into nothing but science fiction and writes sixty science fiction shorts . . . there aren't even sixty markets for that work. If Marketer is lucky, Artist explodes into multiple venues, and is drawing pictures of manta rays, writing romance novels and penning science fiction poems while crafting jewelry with her spare toes. Then she can at least release work to the market in manageable chunks.

It's tempting to make prices cheaper so that Artist will get the work out the door and have more to do, and sometimes that can be the answer. But pricing things too low can cause its own set of problems (discussed later).

Marketer's most common strategy in this case:

1. Select the most common forms of product for one piece of art and arrange those.

2. Arrange for premium versions only for those pieces of art that seem most likely to net those sales, based on sales data, customer surveys and gut instinct.

3. Release items on a schedule to keep from flooding the market and to build a backlog for lean times.

If you want a problem, being too quick at making art is definitely a better problem to have than the opposite.

As you can see, pricing is a complicated exercise. Once Artist's objections have been answered, you have a lot to do:

plans to create, decisions to make, observations to incorporate. Let's move on!

The Three Jaguars Get Practical

omg we love a...

PLAN

It is essential to have a high-level plan for your art business. This plan will allow you to figure out what you need to do to reach your goals and give you the information you need to make snap decisions on pursuing opportunities you might not have time or data to do numbers on.

To make your plan, answer the following questions:

1. How much time do I have? You must be ruthlessly honest answering this question. If you have four hours a week after family and day-job obligations, that's how much time you have. Don't fudge it. Use your weekly number to estimate your yearly work hours.

2. How much do I want to earn? Are you aiming to make full-time money? Grocery money?

3. How much work do I produce on average? Again, be honest. If you only write one novel a year, that's what you write down. If you only get four paintings done a year, write that down. Use last year as an average.

   3a. Do I have enough time to produce the work I have planned? Here's where you find out whether your goal is to get more time or to get more ideas.

4. Are the markets for the products typically produced by my art form particularly vulnerable to technology? While all art is going to have to respond to technological changes, some are positively hammered by them: art, writing and music come to mind.

5. Do I want to aim for the extreme high-end of my market? All art forms have a high-end market, a place inhabited by the absolute masters of the craft (or the marketing). Fine artists might make thousands of dollars a piece; highly-trained musicians might demand the same for a single performance. If you are willing to put in the time and money to reach that pinnacle, and are willing to do the specialized marketing to enter that arena, then note that here.

Now, have a look at your answers and see how they fit together. If you have little time and make few pieces of art, but have the goal of making enough a year to live on, realize that you will either have to change your expectations, find more time to make more work, or aim for the high-end market. If you have a great deal of time but make few pieces of art, then find out why: are you using that time productively? Do you just not have enough ideas?

Get a picture of your work profile. Someone with not many ideas and a lot of time might have the leeway to leap on even vague opportunities, while someone with not much time and too much work to produce might be better served sticking to what they're doing rather than chasing nebulous chances.

Finally, use your high-level plan to estimate how much money an hour you need to make after expenses in order to meet your goal. If you have calculated that you have 520 hours a year and you want to make $30,000, you need to be making about $58 an hour. Keep this number in mind. It is very important!

Now that you have a high-level plan, let's move on to more specific decisions.

Forming a Strategy

The first step to choosing a price for your product is . . . to choose the product you're offering. As we've mentioned before, your piece of art can become any number of products. It's your job to figure out which ones you want to offer . . . and for that, you have to know who you're selling to and the market conditions that you'll be selling in. You can begin by answering these questions:

1. Who is my target market? Does my work appeal to families? Young men? Teen girls? People who like technology? People who consider themselves literary? If you don't already know the answer to this question, you can learn it by observing who buys your work.

2. Where is their money coming from? Once you know who buys your work, figure out how they get income. Single men and women who like to read and like technology are probably earning their own money. Preteens are probably getting it from their parents. It's important to have an idea of how much disposable income your patrons have, because this allows you to plan for whether you'll need one or two of them (affluent patrons without dependents) or hundreds (teen girls with part-time jobs).

3. What else are they buying? Now you need to identify what other things your customers also buy. This helps you identify your competition . . . and your opportunities.

WILD CUSTOMERS

If your teen girl audience is buying both your books and manga, you have to out-compete the manga . . . *or,* you have to expand into that market.

4. Who do you want considered as your competitors? Once you know what you're competing against...ask whether you want to be. Say your art, currently marketed on keychains and stickers, is competing with other tchotchkes . . . and you are only making fifty cents, on average, per sale. Maybe instead you'd prefer to be selling original artwork to collectors, putting you in competition with more rarified artists . . . and netting you the occasional high-ticket sale.

5. What trends do you see in the market? Tablets are exploding and your target market is affluent enough to buy them. Is there some way you can take advantage of that emerging market? Online gaming is a tremendous economic powerhouse, and your younger market segment loves to play them. Is there some way you can tap the same impulse (while avoiding trademark issues!)? Remember: every change is an opportunity.

Once you answer these questions, you should have some notion of the kind of people who buy your work . . . and an idea of what kind of products to market to them.

Case Study 1: High-Volume, Low-Cost Items

For instance. You are an artist drawing cartoon animals. Your work primarily appeals to young people and parents who have children. People in your target audience don't have a lot of discretionary income, which is a bad thing . . . but there are *a lot* of them, which is a good thing. They often buy other items like toys and age-appropriate clothes. Your competitors? Are the giant corporate trademarked characters being sold in every store—something that doesn't cause you anxiety, because by observing your potential customers you know those cartoons often irritate parents who hate their children being sold into the consumer market before they're old enough to talk.

You decide to target the parents who are upset at the lack of choices for non-trademarked character art. They are buying toys, plushes, wall art (which includes murals and wall clings for children to use in their rooms), coloring books and clothes. You decide to investigate these avenues. Your goal: to make merchandise and sell in volume to make up for the low profit-per-unit.

Case Study 2: Low-Volume, High-Cost Items

You like to do calligraphy and are tired of hand-lettering hundreds of envelopes for wedding invitations, which makes you good money but takes you too much time. Your work has broad appeal depending on the subject matter you choose, but it is especially attractive to people for special occasion gifts. Your competitors are other people offering personalized gifts . . . but you believe you can offer a more attractive product by being particularly creative.

You decide to start selling birthday commissions, in which you accept the name of the person and their birthdate and time and offer a variety of add-ons to the piece: "This Day in History," birthstone colors, zodiac information (Chinese/Western), time-of-year information (like autumn themes for

October birthdays), etc. You allow your buyers to customize the piece and charge accordingly, planning to accept far fewer of these commissions, but make more per piece.

Choosing a Product

Once you've decided on a strategy it's time to research your products and assess their production cost. Remember that cost involves (at its highest level) two different expenses:

- **MONEY**. This is the obvious one. If making a plush toy costs you $4 in fabric and $2 in filling and $2 in thread and random bits like buttons for the eyes, then your material cost to make the plush toy is $9. You'll have to charge more than that to make a profit.

- **TIME**. This is the one people often forget. If you have a plush toy that costs $9 to produce and you're charging $12 for it, you are making $3. But say it takes you three hours to make this plush toy. Now you are making a dollar an hour.

Go find the money-per-hour figure you calculated off your high level plan. I'm betting it's higher than a dollar. Our example figure, in fact, was $58. But somehow, you come to the reluctant conclusion that no one is going to pay you $174 . . . plus $9 for the material cost! For a single plush animal. This is why it's important to research costs. Do a prototype, give it a test run . . . go look for the cheapest place to buy the materials you want.

So, keeping costs in mind, research what it would cost to productize your art in the ways you've identified would be most attractive to your target markets. Maybe you've got a lot of administrative assistants who want mousepads, or a lot of smartphone users who want awesome phone backgrounds or independent film-makers who could use soundtracks . . . the possibilities are as endless as your creativity. If running the numbers on one product makes it clear it's not going to work out for you, look into another.

Do this until you've built a portfolio of products and services that you believe you can afford to make, from pretty cool and probably cheap to ultra-premium spiffy.

Now, you are ready to set your prices.

Pricing

You have your material and time costs calculated for everything you want to sell. You have the per-hour number you need to make to hit your target goal. You have a selection of items you'd like to make. You've looked around to see what other people are charging for them. Now it's time to actually do the price-setting.

By this point, you should have an idea of what I'm about to say:

Calculate how much money it costs for you to produce something. Figure out how much time it takes. And then price it to hit the per-hour amount you need to make your target after you add the expenses. Then have a look at the market and see if anyone's selling for around that amount. If you're in the right range, good job! You've got your price.

But wait! you say. What if it doesn't match what's in the market? Like the example above, the plush toy that costs almost $200! What do I do if I have to set my price too high for the market I'm targeting??

You have these choices:

1. Sell something else. This product isn't cost-effective for you; you need to choose products that are.

   But I really want to sell plush toys!

2. All right! If you really want to sell plush toys, find a way to make them cheaper. If the material cost is what's holding you back, find a place that sells your materials for cheaper or in bulk. Or choose cheaper materials. If it's the time spent that's too high, practice making plush toys until you can finish one in half an hour instead of three.

   I've tried those things, and my plush toys still cost too much! But I still really want to sell plush toys!

3. Adjust your expectations of how much money you're going to be making a year. If you can't afford to set your prices to recoup the per-hour cost of your stuffie rabbits, then decide you will make do with making only half the amount a year that you planned. Then you can lower the per-hour cost and get your prices down.

Business for the Right-Brained

But I can't lower that yearly income number . . . I have to make that much to pay the bills!

4. Try outsourcing your labor: find a company that does nothing but produce plush toys and see if they'd be willing to produce yours for you. Be aware that you still have to run numbers on this enterprise: if it takes you an hour to prepare a template for them to use and it costs you $20 to have a prototype sent to you, and if there are set-up fees, etc, etc, all that needs to go into the cost bucket and used to set your prices.

   I can't find anyone to do that! Or at least, not for reasonable money! What do I doooooooo?

5. You can try making your plushes worth $200. Personalize them, or do something crazy like sell your services as entertainment for kids' parties ("Custom plushes made for your birthday girl, to her specifications, at her birthday party in front of her and all her friends!").

   I can't figure out a premium version of my product. Am I out of luck?

6. The last thing you can try is selling your product at the amount you need to get by and seeing if anyone bites. Maybe there *is* a market for your $200 plush toys. You won't know unless you try!

The Psychology of Pricing (Or, What Do You Do After You Start Selling)

So you have a bunch of products. You have set your prices. You start selling.

EVERYONE LOVES A...

Your work is not done.

Now it's time to watch your sales statistics, monitor your customers' reactions and finesse your prices based on your goals. Here are some basic observations on how humans interact with products:

- **Higher Prices = Fewer Sales**

  For the most part, the higher your prices, the fewer people you'll get to buy. This can be handy if, for instance, you have too much work and not enough time. If you are a jewelry-maker and you have more orders than you can handle, increase your prices until you can keep up with demand. This will also have a favorable impact on your bottom line and correctly imply to your potential customers that you are in very high demand.

- **Higher Prices = Expectations of Greater Value/Services**

  As we mentioned earlier in this column, people expect that a higher-priced product will be worth more in some way. Be careful of setting your prices higher than you are willing to back in quality or service. Someone buying a $2000 original should not receive it naked in an otherwise empty envelope, shipped without insurance. If you are not willing to go the extra mile to give $2000 service, don't sell a $2000 product.

On the other hand, if you do offer quality service or premium value, you should increase the price on your product to inform your customers that they will be treated like the kings and queens they are.

(You can also use this particular psychology to increase the perception of value of your product, but we do not recommend inflating your prices in order to make your brand seem more special. Choose a price that you believe your product is worth, that you believe in, and let other people talk you up.)

• Lower Prices/Sales = More Impulse Buys

Lowering the price on a product to below the impulse threshold for that product can help you broaden your audience. People will often buy things they might not ordinarily try if the price is low enough or it's on sale. They might give your work a chance, and this may convert them into a fan.

• Broad Range of Prices = Broad Range of Buyers

As much as possible (and as it is cost-effective for you) you want to offer something for every budget and every level of fan, from the drive-by guests to the casual appreciators to the collectors. It's best not to shut out anyone if you can avoid it. If someone can only give you 99 cents and it costs you very little to make a 99 cent option available, do so.

Caution! When developing products for a broad range of buyers, be sure to differentiate them sufficiently so as not to cut into each other's markets. If you offer a 99 cent song for download, don't make the 10-song album $20 . . . unless it contains album art, singer's notes, or something else to make it worth more as a product than the single download.

- **People Like to Be Generous**
  If at all possible, never put a ceiling on the amount you will accept. Some products lend themselves to "at least $15" style prices, and technology exists to allow customers to enter their own amounts. If you allow them to do so and they like your work, they may often give you more than you ask for.

  Similarly, always give customers a way to express extra appreciation by giving them some way to tip you. It doesn't have to be obtrusive—say, on the front page of your website—but it should be easy to find (a tab on the menu that says 'tip the artist'). Not to say that the front page of your website is a bad place for it. It doesn't matter where your tip mechanism is or how you make it available, so long as you do it.

As you watch your receipts come in, keep an eye on your income. If you aren't earning enough, don't lower your prices immediately; find a new product that you can produce for cheaper or market to a different group of people and see if you can hit your target.

A Sample List of Premium Products

And now, by special request . . . some sample products, with premium versions, for different art disciplines. Please keep in mind these examples do not cover the entire range of awesome marketing ideas, so don't decide because you can't offer the example you can't do any. (And yes, if you like any of the premium ideas, go ahead and use them!).

Web Comic
Basic: Daily strip online.
Premium: Archive of strips yet to be posted, up to two weeks in advance, allowing readers the chance to read what's coming up next.

Fiction
Basic: Selection of cheap short stories available in e-book format.
Premium: Ability to purchase a "ticket" that gives the reader the chance to commission a sequel to one of her favorite short stories.

Art (Digital)
Basic: Downloadable wallpaper.
Premium: Monthly email with attached wallpaper with calendar featuring patron's avatar or game character dressed in different outfits according to the time of year.

Knitting/Crocheting
Basic: Blanket.
Premium: Winter Dorm-Room Package: one blanket, gloves, hat and scarf in a new college attendee's school colors (or fantasy school's, like Hogwarts).

Music
Basic: Single songs available for download.
Premium: Commission to have a song written to the words of a client's poem, with included recording in lossless digital format of the singer performing it.

Card Readings
Basic: Five-card reading in email.
Premium: Five-card reading over patron's choice of email, telephone or in person (within a certain driving radius), with "meditation package" sent to the patron including a stick of incense, a depiction of a card from their reading, and a small tea light.

Poetry

Basic: Physical book of poetry.

Premium: Physical book of poems by the author selected by the client, with special dedication.

Cosplay Costumes

Basic: Clothes to cosplay as the client's favorite character.

Premium: Complete cosplay service, in which you hunt down overseas or specialty vendors for items like wigs, boots and reproductions of special weapons/pins/jewelry.

Jewelry

Basic: Beautiful necklace.

Premium: "Coming of Age" package, where mom buys girl celebrating her puberty a necklace and earrings; she gets to choose her own stones and style to commemorate her coming of age.

Plush Toys

Basic: A single plush toy.

Premium: A one-of-a-kind plush toy made on demand for a child at her birthday party from the materials she selects. (Someone please do this, I would buy it.)

The list here is endless. In fact, the list is so endless that Marketer Jaguar has promptly popped up to say:

As you can see, there are truly few things that can't be productized. Even productizing!

But Wait! (A Small Issue)

But wait! you say. I don't control my own pricing!

For various reasons, you may not have the ability to set your own prices, probably because you are selling through an intermediary and part of your contract allows them to change the retail prices. If you don't control your own pricing, it is still important to be aware of all the things we've spoken of.

Why?

1. So you can agitate your business partner into staying responsive to the market. If you sign a contract with someone allowing them to sell a product based on your artwork, you are their business partner, not their supplicant. It is imperative to treat the relationship like a partnership, request explanations, do audits, ask for changes. Art is your passion and the mainstay of your spirit. But your products are your livelihood and represent your best chance at making

a living at what you're doing. No one will care about your passion and your profit and your ability to make a living the way you will, so don't let your business partners off the hook. Be your own advocate.

That's the first reason you should remain aware of pricing. The second, of course, is:

2. . . . so you can jump ship if your business partner makes consistently poor decisions. A business partner that does not treat you like a full equal in that partnership, who doesn't listen to or respond to your reasonably-presented concerns, your sales data or your ideas should be left behind the moment your contract allows it. Remember: no one cares about your livelihood the way you do. So if you can't make someone see eye-to-eye on something that is impacting your ability to earn an income, leave them and find someone willing to engage you as an equal.

Epilogue

If you are to take away anything from this chapter, we would draw your attention back to the separation of art from product. Your art is not the product; it is not worth the money its products get on the market. It will always be something more sublime than money can describe with a price tag. The artist who doesn't understand this distinction will always be a resentful beggar: on one hand, feeling angry that her art isn't "worth more" and resenting the patrons who don't pay her enough, and on the other feeling like she is importuning anyone she asks for money because art doesn't seem to have a price. The transaction ceases to be between someone producing something and offering it for sale . . . and becomes one where the artist is selling her soul and hating people for not thinking it's worth more than a cup of coffee.

Remember: once you put a price tag on something, it ceases to be about your heart and becomes about the way it gets into the hands of other people. Give the business of pricing to Marketer and Business Manager and send Artist back to her studio, and everyone will be much happier.

In conclusion: stay aware of your own unexamined assumptions. Question yourself constantly. Watch the market; poll your customers. Remember that the art is not the product and that financial success has no bearing on artistic merit. Reassure yourself that changing prices to reflect market realities and to adjust for demand, expectation and even your own short-term and long-term goals is okay. And then go forth and play. The economy is a big experiment, and art lends itself fabulously to high-premium productizing. You have very little to lose and a great deal to learn!

Communication

RELATIONSHIPS ARE THE building blocks of business. We all know it . . . how many times have we heard something like 'It's who you know'? Or maybe 'they got where they are because they're friends with x'? Or even 'You've gotta network'? Usually these things are said with a sneer, as if it's more important to be talented than it is to be good with people. But the Three Jaguars are here to tell you that there are hundreds of thousands of talented people who are also unsuccessful. It takes more than talent to make it. If the definition of professional success is "enough people buy my work that I can make a living off of it," then obviously, people are part of the equation. No people, no audience. No audience, no money.

Suddenly it makes a little more sense why "it's who you know" is such a common phrase. It takes more than one person to make a career out of your talent: not just your fans, but people who work to make your art available to them in any number of ways; and not just them, but even other artists, who are your peers and a place to turn to for advice and an understanding ear.

And the key to all these relationships? Is communication.

Ah, communication. So many ways to strengthen relationships . . . and so many ways to wreck them. You need to do a lot of communicating as a creative businessperson. Let's get started.

Communicating with Fans and Customers and Patrons: Marketer

Our first target? Your fans, customers, and patrons. Some of you may remember from the chapter on roles that Marketer is your customer-facing self . . .

But wait! Shouldn't ARTIST be the one talking with fans? They're fans of the art, after all?

Maybe so, but with rare exception, Artist is very sensitive to other people's interpretations of her work. Too sensitive. Criticism offends or depresses her; lukewarm responses inspire doubt or resentment. Enthusiasm gets her talking . . . maybe too much, draining her interest in finishing the work, or revealing spoilers fans weren't quite ready for, or distracting her so much she doesn't spend any time doing anything productive.

No, Artist needs to be in the studio. Marketer is the only one with the aplomb and savvy to handle fans . . . who are, after all, also your customers, and entitled to their negative opinions and complaints as well as their enthusiasms.

So here's the watchword for communicating with fans and customers: **service**.

Why?

Because your fans and customers and patrons are all supporting your creative endeavors. Whether it's through their enthusiasm, their word-of-mouth recommendations or their dollars, they are participating in your career directly, by giving you free advertising (and the best kind according to studies), by funding you, and by cheering you on. They don't have to do any of those things; you're only one of many thousands of artists they could be supporting, but they've chosen you! So your job is to make them glad they're spending their time and attention on your work: by comporting yourself with respect for them and ensuring that they are pleased with the quality of the products they are selecting to get your work into their hands.

Remember: your art, when it trades hands, is a product.

Even if you're posting it for free, that free download or web-page or sample is still a product, which means Marketer is the one in charge of packaging it, making it available, and dealing with people's responses to it. Artist is going to be verrrrrrrry tempted to butt into this relationship, but she doesn't belong here.

So let's talk specifics.

How Do I Talk to Customers?

Some principles first:

1. **Be interested.**

   These are people who are interested in your work; it behooves you to be interested in them. Listen to their response to what you're creating. Listen to their experiences when they buy something from you. Tell yourself 'I will react to all this later, for now, I will pretend like they're talking about someone else's work, not mine.'

   Did something touch them? Why? Make notes. Artist did something right; she'll want to know.

   Did they really love the product? Was the print perfectly trimmed? Was the mug exactly what they asked for? Were the extra graphics in the e-book appreciated? This is valuable information for Marketer.

   Did the buying experience please them? Was it easy for them to pay? Did they get what they wanted in a timely fashion? Were they pleased with the level of interaction they had with you or your distributor? This is information Marketer and Business Manager need to manage relationships with business partners (or to streamline your own processes).

Remember: people who like your work have at least one thing in common with you, and probably a lot more. Be interested in them, because they will be interesting people, and they have valid and useful things to say.

2. Be professional.

Most of us have heard terrible stories about Artists Behaving Badly on the internet. You don't want to be one of those people, because those stories spread like wildfire and repairing the damage afterward is painful and will make Marketer weep.

You are a businessperson now; you have a license that says so. Be professional. That means be courteous, listen to what people are saying, and above all, don't get emotional about it. If you absolutely must have an emotional reaction, have one in private, unload it on your friends and confidants, or write it down and then trash the letter. If you are prone to emotional responses, try not to use communication media that reveal it: avoid phones, and never send emails immediately; wait a day before responding.

3. Be kind.

Everyone remembers kindness, and everyone needs it. If you're following the guidelines above, you're already

interested, and you're already professional. Being courteous and thoughtful is icing on the cake.

And everyone loves cake.

So, having set out some basic rules, let's look at some details.

Staying In Contact: Managing Your Inbox

Most of us are going to need to instate some rules to deal with
fan communications. If you don't have too many emails now
to handle, don't worry: you will. It's best to set up some rules
for yourself initially so you can manage your customer's expectations as well as keep yourself from pulling out your hair.
Try these:

**1. Establish an email specifical-
ly for contact from customers.**

Make this email different from the one you use for personal communication (no mixing up Mom's birthday
party invitation with someone's request that you mail
them a print). If you're super-fancy-good with email,
you can set up a rule that
routes your business
partner emails into a
separate folder, or flags
and labels them. If you're
not super-fancy-good
with email, use a sep-
arate email address
for your business part-
ners, so you can manage

those relationships without being distracted by dozens of fan comments on your latest offering.

1a. If you work primarily by phone, by all means, get a separate phone number for your business.

2. Batch your responses.

As tempting as it is to loom over your inbox like a hungry vulture, checking email can become a spasmodic reflex that interferes with you doing anything else. Decide right now when you're going to answer your customer responses, whether it's email or voice mail or social media, and do it all at once. Most of you will want to do it once or twice a day (maybe at lunch/day's end). You can also do it biweekly or weekly, whichever suits your work-mode better. Whatever you do, though, choose a block of time and stick to it. This leads you to . . .

3. Office Hours.

It's important to maintain communication with your customers. Nothing is more irritating than ordering a product and not receiving it, and not getting any explanation about why it hasn't arrived. You want to remain available to help your customers and answer their questions, and also to answer as many fan responses as you can manage . . . but you don't want to lose your work-time to it either. Once you've decided on a reasonable amount of time, and time period, for answering customer responses, post your "office hours" somewhere people will see them. Explain that you will be checking email once a day at this time, and that you will be in the studio otherwise and appreciate people's patience—if you're not working, you're not producing wonderful new things to share!

Do this even if your work is on a computer. It's especially tempting for writers, digital artists, and other computer-using creatives to sneak a peek at their email or do a quick refresh on the blog to see if anyone's said anything lately. Don't! Close everything but the program you need to do your work and keep your eyes on the prize. If you're bad at this, there are several programs that will lock down your computer's shiny things for you so you can't check until a certain time. Use them.

Templates (or Getting the Most Out of Your Response Time)

Most of us will get very similar kinds of questions from fans and customers. "Do you sell a print of x?" or "Do you offer electronic versions of that book" or "Where can I find your jewelry in person," etc, etc. The questions will be specific to your art form, but if you've been working for a while you'll know exactly what I'm talking about, and have a list of those questions in your head. Write them down now!

Did you do it?

All right. Now, write a FAQ answering those questions and post it somewhere people can see it.

Hooray! You have reached about 10% of the people who will want to know something. The rest of them will still be sending you email or asking you in some other way directly. For those people, create a template answering the question. For instance, in response to 'can I buy a paper version of your e-book':

Thanks for your interest in [Book Name]! At this time, [Book Name] is scheduled to hit print on [Date]. You can preorder it now from [Name of Store 1] or [Name of Store 2], or you can pick it up when it arrives in stores on [Date again].

If you'd like to follow my publication news more closely, you can also follow me on twitter at [name], check my Facebook profile [name], or follow my blog [here].

Thank you again!

You can have a separate template for books that aren't due to hit print for whatever reason. Make a folder of these and keep them handy so you can cut and paste them into your messages. If you work primarily by phone, use scripts for the same purpose.

Keep an eye on your tone in these responses. You are aiming for friendly, courteous and professional; not personal, emotional or obsequious. As social creatures we are highly attuned to the suggestion of desperation, and a desperate-sounding business person makes people nervous: no one wants to be the target of hard-selling, or have their arms twisted by pity.

Doing Good When You Do Bad

The most important time to be good at communication is when something's gone wrong . . . particularly when it's your fault. As we mentioned previously in the Inner Customer chapter, the only way to transform a negative situation into a positive one is through superlative customer service. Here are the most common issues, and how to deal with them:

You Delivered Late (or Not at All)

You took on a commission, or promised to deliver something on schedule . . . and life interfered, or you hated the project. Your instinct is to curl into a ball in a dark corner and hope the fan doesn't notice, or the customer will wait to complain until you can fix it.

The worst thing you can do is stop talking. If you see in advance you're going to be late, contact the customer now and explain that there's been a hold-up and you won't be able to deliver on time. If you're just barely going to miss the deadline, apologize; if you're going to miss it by a huge margin, offer recompense. Imagine yourself as that customer and think about what it would take to make you feel like you've been treated fairly, and do that, whether it's a partial or full refund, a coupon toward other services, or some other brainstorm.

If you're on schedule and something happens the day of the deadline, then again, talk to the customer and explain the delay.

In either case, make a new deadline with milestones and tell your customer as you reach them so they feel comfortable that you are actually working on their product or project. Whatever you do, don't stop communicating with your customer. You should be more communicative with them as you make errors, not less. Many people will forgive you for being late if you explain what's going on and deliver on your new schedule. What they won't forgive is being left in the dark with a broken promise.

Can you blame them?

The Product Was Messed Up

Closely related to missing a deadline is dealing with product problems. Someone's print is on flimsy paper, that person's e-book formatting is full of errors, yet another fan's hand-painted glass ornament arrived in pieces. When dealing with product problems, first identify who was responsible. Are you the one making the product? If so, you're the one who gets to troubleshoot and fix it.

Was it someone else's issue, because you licensed the product to them? Then you have to figure out where the responsibility lies. Did you give your distributor a flawed file, or bad directions? Or was it solely their issue? Once you figure it out, you can either handle it yourself, or you can tell the customer to contact the distributor.

Take notes on this process so you don't repeat your

mistakes. If someone loses their $2000 brooch in the mail, re-quire your clients to purchase insurance, or to go through a different mail provider.

Fan Didn't Like the Art

And here is the one time you have permission to . . . SAY NOTHING.

And really, you shouldn't. There will be people who dis-like what you do for any number of reasons. Some might go so far as to hate it with fire. Your job, when faced with these people, is not to say a word. Don't comment on the negative review. Don't answer the snarky blog post. Don't make your own oblique but easily-guessed comments on social media about fans not getting it.

If you are cornered in public by someone saying some-thing about how bad your work is, and are forced to answer, just say politely, "I'm sorry to hear that," and move on. Art is subjective. Not everyone is going to like it, and that's okay.

What's not okay is an artist getting on someone's case because their tastes are different from yours.

Please note "fan not liking the art" is different from "fan complaining about the product." If someone says they hate your jewelry because it falls apart easily, make sure your jewelry doesn't fall apart. Make sure theirs in particular hasn't, by offering to examine and fix/replace it. (See above, Product Was Messed Up.) But if they say your jewelry "sucks because it's trite and kitschy," then you are good to ignore them.

Sample Responses

Marketer Jaguar says: "Let's review!"

Positive Situation: Fan is Happy!

- "I'm glad you enjoyed it! I'm working on the next book in that series now, focusing on Character Y from the first novel."

- "Thank you! That particular piece took x hours, and I learned a great deal from it. I'm hoping I can apply it to my next piece."

- "That's great to hear! Was there anything in particular you liked? Could I offer any options to make it more special?"

Neutral Situation: Fan is Indifferent.

- "If you liked the romantic elements of that story but it didn't really satisfy, I write romances under a pen name . . . here's a coupon for 10% off, give it a try."

- "Yeah, I know it's been a while since I've put out a new design, but I'm working on something really special . . . I expect it to be ready in a month. Would you like to be on a mailing list to see sneak peeks?"

- "I see that particular product didn't wow you . . . can you tell me what about it was subpar?"

Negative Situation: Fan is Angry!

- "I'm sorry to hear you didn't enjoy it."

- "How did I fail to meet your expectations? Is there something I can do to make it right?"

- *[crickets chirping]*

Don't Do or Say This:

- "You don't like my art, you suck!"

- "I'm having problems, please give me money!"

- "That reviewer is wrong, I'm going to explain why!"

- "That person said something cruel, I think I will tell my fans and let them go after her."

So, we've dealt (effectively, we hope!) with fans and customers and patrons. Let's move on to the next set of people. This business of communication, it never ends . . .

Communicating with Business Partners: Business Manager

As an artist running your own business, you're going to need to interface with a lot of people in pursuit of your business goals. Banks, coordinators, agents, freelancers, corporate buyers, gallery owners and venue operators, licensing officials and distributors . . . the list goes on and on. You can minimize your contact with people outside your studio, but your business will die quickly without partnerships. It doesn't matter if you're writing books or making costumes, you will need supplies, business licenses and people to help you get your work into the right hands.

The proper person to manage these relationships is Business Manager. She's the one with the account books and an understanding of the bottom line. She's the one who'll be able to evaluate these partners on their performance: are they doing the job? Are they doing it well? Is it worth the hassle/expense to maintain the partnership? What have they done for you?

So here's the watchword for communicating with business partners: **equality.**

Why? Because you are not a beggar. Too many artists set up their own businesses and then continue thinking of themselves as individuals with brushes and keyboards, hoping to get people to like their stuff. Once you start paying taxes, you are no longer just the Artist; you're a small businessperson, running your own enterprise. You don't need other people's charity; you are making money, and you're looking for people to help you do it . . . people who will not so incidentally get a share of your profit. Repeat these things after the Jaguars:

YOU ARE NOT BOTHERING ANYONE!

YOU DON'T GET TO DECIDE WHEN YOU ARE, EITHER. THAT'S THEIR CHOICE. SO RESPECT THEM AND LET THEM MAKE IT.

Have you got that? Put it on your wall. You are not a charitable cause. You do not need to beg for people's money or help. You are there to present a case on why doing business with you is a good risk. They get to decide whether to take that chance.

Let's talk about specifics.

Networking

One of the first places Artist fails in business communication is networking . . . because she is too aware of the importance of other people, and wonders why they should choose to talk to her instead of some other artist. This worry drains away all her natural brilliance and makes her look timid and desperate, and no one likes the scent of desperation. So as tempting as it is to have Artist show up to network with business contacts . . . send her back to the studio. Marketer and Business Manager work together at networking events; Business Manager evaluates the crowd and decides who should be approached, and Marketer goes off to be shiny and excited at them . . . with Business Manager at her shoulder to keep her from getting carried away. (Marketer and Artist have a tendency to promise things in the heat of the moment that they should probably have thought through more carefully, so make sure Business Manager is riding herd on them whenever they're out.)

Your goal at networking events, whether it's a party or a convention or a fair, is to think of everyone as a potential partner. A potential partner, not a victim, not a godlet who would never be interested in you, and not a target to be hunted down. These are all people, business people like you, who

may or may not have something to offer, and what you're seeking is a mutually beneficial business relationship.

The jaguars cannot emphasize enough how important it is to keep a clear perspective on people at networking events. So here are some principles for networking:

1. **Be interested.**

   Sound familiar? The people at networking events are involved in the same things you are, and that gives you a great deal in common. Additionally, they are involved in segments of the business you might not be. The layout specialist knows things about books you don't as a writer (unless you also do layout!), and might pass some fascinating stories and tips to you. The maintainer of the famous cosplay blog can tell you what kinds of posts got the most attention, and what kind of things she thinks are newsworthy. The lighting expert can tell you what kind of effects are possible on stage and which look ridiculous or cost too much. Ask about what someone does and be interested in their answers. Learn as much as you can. Share your own experiences in kind—

2. **Don't Make it All About You**

   —but don't take over the conversation and talk about your latest awesome, whatever that was. Don't talk about how brilliant you are, either, and nothing else. Don't go into monologue mode and don't try to sell yourself.

   But wait! Isn't that the point of networking?

No! The point of networking is to find good relationships. Relationships exist between two people . . . that means you and someone else. Not just you. If you spend all your time talking yourself up, you'll never have the chance to evaluate someone else's talents and personality. You're looking for a good fit for your needs and your style. The highest-power distributor in the entire room might be someone who hates methodical workers—what if you're one of them? Even if you manage to interest that person into signing you on, they'll never be as invested in your success as the medium-sized distributor who's looking for dependable, less volatile artists. That person might be very excited to work with you, and do a lot more for you, and you would never have known because you were too busy talking about yourself to listen.

3. Don't Be Catty.

The other powerfully helpful thing you can do about yourself is . . . don't talk about other people. Unless you admire them! But don't expose any of your secret doubts, fears, or jealousies. Nothing turns someone off more than hearing an artist tear down another artist. It hints at the kind of emotional instability that leads to prima donna behavior, and no one wants to deal with a prima donna when they can go with someone more sensible. Be professional, be courteous. Never say cruel or mean things about other artists. It's a good idea anyway, for your emotional health. It just also happens to be good for your reputation.

If you do admire other artists, feel free to mention them now and then when the conversation is appropriate. Doing so demonstrates that you have enough self-confidence not to be threatened by other people's success. Nothing says 'winner' like someone who doesn't have to tear other people down to feel good or get ahead.

4. Pay Attention to Your Peers.

If you approach a likely person and discover they're not a potential business contact, but rather an Artist in search of them like yourself . . . don't cut them off. Apply the same principles you would to a potential business partner: be interested, don't make it all about you, don't be catty, and get their business card. They may have had experiences you can learn from . . . they might even become friends.

But wait! This all feels very Machiavellian. Aren't I being disingenuous here?

Not at all. You are putting your best foot forward, and disciplining yourself to be courteous, friendly and interested. You are learning from other people, listening to them, and keeping yourself from saying mean things (which is, after all, something our mothers have been telling us to do since we were old enough to talk). The reason that acting this way is good for your reputation is because it's the behavior of someone thoughtful, mature and with some self-control. Your goal is to be that thoughtful, mature and self-disciplined person, and let your reputation take care of itself. But being that way takes work, and the work sounds to jaundiced ears like putting on a mask. It's not. It's practicing being a good businessperson, and a good person.

Contrary to popular belief, that does require practice. So don't put it off!

Following Up

So you've done some networking, gotten some names . . .

. . . and this is where people usually stop. They manage the first part of networking, opening the channel . . . but they never follow through. Almost invariably this is due to a lack of confidence, or a desire not to bother someone.

Think you're not doing one of these things? Have you ever thought the following:

> 'Oh, this project isn't quite right for them.'
> 'I'm not ready to pitch this one, I'll get back to them when I am.'

All of these interior comments are signs of procrastination. Repeat after Marketer:

Once again: you must stop thinking like an Artist. When your work becomes your job, you need to ping your contacts to see if they're interested in what you're doing, so you have a sense of whether you're going to have a market for it before you're done. Nor can you do someone's job for them. If you have an editor who likes fantasy, and your fantasy has modern elements, or romantic ones . . . let the editor decide if she wants to look at it. You don't have to read someone's mind before you ask them if they're interested. Don't let yourself get in your own way. Don't tell yourself you're not ready; if you're not ready now, you never will be, because it's not about your confidence in the project, it's about your confidence in whether someone else will want it. And the only way to resolve that question . . . is to find out.

Send that email, pick up the phone. Write out a script if you're going to be talking on the phone, it will help with the shakes. Make a template for the email. Something like this:

> *Dear Networking Contact:*
>
> *We met at Function X, where we discussed [something interesting/memorable]. I have a project that might suit your [product line/catalog/label/imprint/ etc]. It's a [short description of product: one phrase or sentence at most]. I've attached a [sample/synopsis/ photo/etc]. Tell me if it looks like a good fit.*
>
> *Yours,*
>
> *Business Manager*

Notice that nowhere in this letter do we mention whether the project is finished. If your business contact isn't interested, then there's no rush. If he is, well . . . there's incentive for you to finish. If you're close to finished, put in a few all-nighters. If it's going to be longer than a week, send a partial to the contact so they can decide whether they want to go forward with it.

Whatever you do, don't let those business contacts lie fallow. You acquired them for a reason.

Maintaining the Relationship without a Project

. . . *but wait!* You don't have a project you could pitch them. At all!

There's no reason not to keep a line open to someone even if you don't have a project to pitch them. Maybe you're between albums, or you're retooling to do a new style of jewelry, or you're taking half a year off to do research and continued education. That doesn't mean your contact doesn't have useful information you might want. Maybe you've run into a fabric supplier and taken their number, and you're not currently buying to make costumes . . . but you run into some new fabric on some website and want to know more about it. Why not ask? Your contact has the expertise. The layout freelancer you shook hands with at a convention; even if you don't have a job for him, he might be willing to answer your questions about font choices and book packaging. The editor who buys fantasy might be able to tell you who to contact to buy romance.

Your networking contacts are not cardboard cut-outs whose only talents are helping you with specific projects. They are part of a business ecosystem, complex and interwoven. If you cut yourself off from their entire expertise, you are missing out on a vast fund of knowledge and goodwill and opportunity. Plus, they probably enjoy talking about the esoterica of their profession with someone who's honestly interested!

So stop neglecting your contacts. And remember, if someone contacts you to ask you about something . . . that's your chance to become a valued part of the network.

. . . and from here, we pause for an important digression.

Business for the Right-Brained

Positive Language

One of the most difficult things for Artists to learn is the art of positive business language. Their lack of self-confidence often sabotages them: they either go the route of being too self-effacing and use weak language that makes them sound like poor risks; or they go in the opposite direction and talk about themselves constantly, declaring that of course you will love them because they are brilliant, and turn off just about everyone.

Positive business language is neither self-aggrandizing or self-deflating. It is confident, friendly and professional. Compare the following:

> *"Here's my stuff. Um, yes, that's $5. I know it's a lot, but it costs $3 to make . . ."*

. . . with:

> *"Hi, how are you? Ah, yes, those are $5. I also have a lower-cost option over here at $2, if you like stickers. If you want to see the image better, check out these posters."*

Or these two:

> *"I just finished this . . . it's not as good as I hoped it would be, but at least it's finished."*

. . . versus:

> *"Here's my latest piece. I learned a great deal from it,*

which I hope to apply to my next project, already on my work table."

Your job is not to apologize for being an artist or for your work. You should not be embarrassed to ask for your prices, should not belabor your mistakes or errors—you can admit them if asked, or you must admit them if they're related to a product mix-up, but you shouldn't beat yourself about them in public. You shouldn't think of yourself as a beggar when approaching business partners or customers. You are offering something of value to people who might be interested, or not, and both cases are okay and normal and good.

The number one thing to avoid in your language is deciding in advance what someone is going to feel and telling them. For two reasons: first, it's rude! You don't know whether someone is going to like or dislike something; telling them will not convince them of your telepathy, it will irritate them. Secondly, particularly when it's a negative feeling, it has a chance of influencing them to agree with you. If you tell someone 'it's not very good, I made a lot of mistakes . . .' then you have primed them to look for mistakes. In fact, they will seek the mistakes before they even see the piece. Don't prejudge the work for someone else. Tell them 'here it is' and grant them the right to make their own judgment. Without your help.

Sealing the Deal: Contracts

So you've made a decision to do business with someone, whether that person's a contractor, a bank, a distributor,

another company, a friend who freelances.

Get a contract/agreement.

Read the contract/agreement.

There is no substitute for these steps. Like other kinds of relationships, business partnerships benefit from knowing where the boundaries are and what each party's expectations are. Happy, long-lasting relationships are sustained by communication and clear understanding of responsibilities. The contract will help both of you set out those responsibilities and expectations so that no one is surprised by anything, or uncomfortable doing the labor/exchanging the goods and services.

But wait! What if you're dealing with a friend?

The jaguars know it seems painful to ask a friend to sign a contract, but it's still the safest way to keep things on track. If it makes you feel better, don't call it a contract . . . call it a list of deliverables, or a schedule. Put something down in writing that makes it clear what you are giving one another . . . or be prepared not to count on it to happen.

Which is fine, if you're willing to let things go if they don't happen. If it is important, though, we encourage you to either get that agreement . . . or pay someone to do it on time, and according to your needs.

If you are accepting an agreement from a company, read the agreement and make sure you understand it. Check out a book from the library on contract law if you want to figure it out yourself, or ask your business partner for clarification if you don't understand something in the agreement. If the document is long and complicated enough, consider hiring a legal aide for an hour to have a look with you and teach you what something means. Make sure that legal aide is conversant in that particular kind of law; a child custody lawyer won't understand the nuances in a book contract the way a Intellectual Property law specialist will.

If the deal still looks good to you after reading the contract, sign it.

If it doesn't, *negotiate.*

That's right. Who said you have to accept something as-is? Some types of business won't allow negotiation, but it never hurts to ask. For most creative business partnerships, however, negotiation is expected. Check off some items that you want revised or discussed and go forth to discuss them. Before you go into that discussion, have your counter-offers prepared, and consider what kinds of compromises you're prepared to make. Make a list of your priorities and goals, and be ready to evaluate whether a compromise suggested in the meeting or follow-up will still meet those priorities and goals. If it doesn't, say so.

Most business partners will be willing to negotiate, particularly if there's some give-and-take: you compromise on some things to get the things you really want; they do the same. But if after negotiation you still don't like the contract . . . walk away.

Did you really expect the jaguars to say otherwise?

In the end, this is your art, and your livelihood. No one is going to care about it the way you do. You owe it to yourself to fight for fair treatment and for the goals you want to achieve. Never believe that you need to cage yourself into the prison of a bad contract 'because that's the only way you can make it.' Say no, and use that self-respect to find a different way. There's always a different way. Even if you have to chart the course yourself.

So, we've dealt (effectively, we hope!) with fans, customers and patrons. We moved on to business partners. In this final segment of our communication chapter, Artist finally gets her chance to speak . . .

Communicating with Peers: Artist

Finally, Artist gets to talk! No doubt she was getting frustrated sitting in the corner. Marketer didn't want her talking to fans lest she become an Artist Behaving Badly in the press. Business Manager didn't want her talking to business partners lest she come across as pathetic and underconfident. But finally, among peers she can be herself!

Mostly. It's still easy for Artist to get in trouble, particularly if she's plagued by insecurities (as so many of us are). There are artists who are doing better than we are—whether it's financially or artistically—that might incite our envy and self-doubt; there are artists who are not as good as we are that tempt us to make snippy comments about how far they have to go, or how they only wish they were where you were.

So how to navigate these pitfalls? Keep the watchword for peer relationships in mind: **fellowship**.

Why fellowship? Because you were once a newbie artist

yourself. And one day you might become that hyper-successful artist you admire. But every artist is on a path, and you're all traveling it together. Your goal is to become the graceful artist who helps the new people (the way she would have liked to be helped back then) and takes notes from the more experienced ones, while capable of sharing her own experiences, lessons learned and enthusiasms with others.

So let's deal with some practicalities.

How to Deal with Jealousy (and Envy, and Discouragement, and . . .)

We might as well start with the elephant in the room, the issue most of us will struggle with and no one wants to admit to. That artist over there is making more money. The artist next door has more fame. And that artist over there is so much more talented we want to crawl into a hole and never come out.

It's inevitable that most of us will have these moments. If we're lucky they really are moments, brief thoughts that come and go . . . if we're not, they're soundtracks we hear over and over in our head, comparing us unfavorably to other people and either ragging on ourselves for it, or wishing ill things on other people. So what to do?

The three Jaguars have no easy answer for this one, alas. Or we do, but it's a somewhat painful one:

And that's really the truth of us as artists. We grieve, we suffer, we rage, and the best place to deal with all that is the studio, where we can transform it into something more productive. Still, there's only so much time you can spend in the studio; eventually you have to walk outside, if only for groceries. And if you vanish too completely into your work, you won't have access to the people who really do understand you: how you work, what you care about so much, and what your struggles are. You *want* to get out to talk to others! And those angers and insecurities can get in the way. So here are some step-by-steps for dealing with negative feelings inspired by your peers:

1. **Keep it to yourself.**

   No one wants to hear bad things about someone else. No one ever has, or there wouldn't be fables about foxes and grapes that have survived for centuries. Don't get a reputation for pettiness. It's terrible for PR, and to be honest, it's no good for your spirit either. You might think talking other people down helps you, but all it does is shape you into the kind of person who needs to hurt other people to feel good.

Remember, you are the tool you use to bring your art into the universe. Don't sully the brush.

2. Practice positive thinking.

Yeah, yeah, you say. We've heard this one before. But not the way the jaguars suggest. Instead of looking at a more successful artist and thinking, 'I hate them! I wish they would fail!' (very bad) or 'they're nice people, they deserve their success' (typical, but what are we, saints?) think instead . . . 'hey, they're successful . . . maybe I can learn something from them. Or ask them for advice.' The writer who's faster at writing novels . . . maybe they'd be willing to tell you how they do it. Or the musician who seems to have booked a thousand gigs could tell you how he got started. Instead of looking at other artists as competition, think of them as allies and resources. Instead of thinking of other people's success as a threat, think of it as an opportunity to learn something that you could use.

Don't worry: you don't have to become someone else to learn something useful from them. Even if you decide that the successful novelist's tips for writing faster won't work for you, just considering the ideas will probably bring you to a better understanding of your own process and priorities.

Remember:

3. Do the work.

In the end the best anodyne for discouragement, fear, envy and jealousy is . . . to do more work. Your work, the work that nourishes you. Returning to your art and immersing yourself in it will not only help you feel more accomplished (and get more accomplished), it will remind you that what other people are doing is not relevant. The only thing that matters is you and the work. Let the art itself reset your perspective, and remind you that there are more important things than whether someone else has t-shirts in the mall.

Fame is fleeting, money comes and goes. The feeling you get when you sit down to make something . . .

that will always be yours, true, and eternal.

In the end, the only way to deal with negative feelings is to practice fostering positive ones. Make no mistake, this does take practice. But the more you concentrate on positive actions and words, the more your thoughts will fall in line. Let's move on to some positive communicative acts for our peers.

Paying It Forward

One of the most important concepts in the art social ecosystem is also one of the oldest in disguise; we call it "paying it forward," but the world knows it as a version of the golden rule.

Paying it forward is the acknowledgment that someone helped us when we were confused and new to something, and so it's our job to turn around and help someone else. And if you were so unlucky as to never have had that help, then paying it forward is your way of saying, "I refuse to let someone else go through what I did, and struggle alone."

There are a lot of ways to pay it forward, but most of them involve answering questions and demonstrating things you've learned to other people. You can do this in email, on forums, in person at shows or during meet-ups. Anyplace you're gathered with your peers, virtually or physically, there's an opportunity to show kindness to someone who has a question, or make a suggestion when someone reveals their frustrations to you. You can do it as formally or casually as you like: if you prefer structured time, you might give a free seminar at the high school or college you graduated from, or if you'd rather something more casual you could simply give advice to someone at a party (who has asked for it: unwanted advice is a Bad Thing). Get into the habit of kindness, and choose as many forms of paying it forward as you can manage.

But wait! You say. I don't have time to help a lot of people!

The three jaguars are sympathetic. There will come a point in the career of even a modestly successful artist when you will be receiving more mail and more attention than you can possibly field while still getting any work done. It's not necessary to martyr yourself to pay it forward, and no one would ask you to. As you grow more pressed for time (or more stressed), limit your activities to the number of charitable acts you can handle. Maybe you can't give a free talk at the bookstore about independent publishing without cutting too badly into your writing time, or answer all the emails you get about the topic. But you could maybe write a FAQ about it and leave it on your website, and in the future you can direct people looking for help there.

Remember: do unto others what you'd have them do unto you. And that brings us neatly to . . .

Asking for Advice

. . . the other end of the spectrum, when you're the one who needs help. One of the most useful skills you can cultivate is how to learn from other people, and how not to be afraid to ask them about how they got to where they are. Most of us are convinced that successful people have no time for us, or wouldn't want to bother talking to us, or don't want to share their secrets, and that might be true of some slim number of them. But most artists like talking about their work and are flattered that someone might want their opinion (wouldn't you be?). So don't let the handful of nasty curmudgeons discourage you. There's a lot your peers can teach you if you're willing to ask. Here are some basic tips:

1. Be courteous.

Remember, you are a stranger asking someone for advice. Don't demand help, and don't act like you expect to be indulged. Be casual and friendly, and not familiar. Try openers like, "I really admire the way you x . . . how did you do it?" or "Your newest work was a big success! How did you get so many people in the door at the opening?"

Even if the person you're approaching is someone you already know, it's still good to be polite.

2. Be specific.

It's hard for someone to help you if you don't know what you want help on. Worse, a nebulous question suggests that the conversation might drag on. If you want to know how someone writes three novels a year, that's what you should ask about . . . and if the conversation rambles on past that, then all the better. But have in mind at least a few things you want to learn before you approach someone.

3. Don't talk about yourself if you can at all avoid it.

Your goal is to get your peer to tell you something you don't know, so you want to keep the conversation focused on them: their work process, their style, their business practices, their methodologies, their techniques. Whatever it is you want to know, ask them about it and let them talk. If necessary, you can mention your specific problem: "I can't seem to get my hems to stop gapping, do you have any advice on how to flatten them out?" But don't turn it into an advertisement. "My latest book isn't selling many copies and

I don't know what to do," is acceptable. A long digression on your book, why it's awesome, why you can't fathom why it's not selling, mentioning its title prominently isn't. You're there to learn, not to advertise. If at the conclusion of the conversation, your peer wants to know more about your work . . . then you hand over the business card or URL.

4. Watch for Signals That Your Conversation Partner is Done

The most gracious thing you can learn is when to stop. Few people practice this one, reasoning that their goal is to get information and if they stop before they've gotten it, what's the point? But pressing your peers for advice is not the same as pressing a business partner for results. Your business partners are under contract with you to deliver something, and if they fail or if they look like they're failing, it's your job to figure out what's going on. But your peers are under no such obligation, and pressing them when they want to be free of the conversation will result in you getting a reputation for being creepy or obnoxious. And then no one will want to talk to you.

So, get used to signs that someone might be done with you. In person, twitching, fidgeting or someone's eyes frequently moving away from you are good signs. Or if they say things that sound like closers: "I'll be sure to get back to you about that," or "that's true, it's been nice talking to you." If the person talking with you changes their pattern: if they were talking a great deal, for instance, and are now saying "I see" or "yeah" every once in a while, they may be tired of the conversation. Be polite and disengage: "It was nice talking to you," or "Thanks for the tips, they were really helpful," or "Well, all this talking has made me parched, I think I'm ready for a refill." At that point, if it was a good conversation, ask for a card, or exchange cards, and go.

In email and chat, long pauses or delays between replies are signs that someone either doesn't want to continue the conversation, or is being distracted to the point that they shouldn't be expected to continue. This is not necessarily a reflection on you or the conversation, merely on the fact that virtual conversations are often asynchronous, and you should expect them to be prone to interruption. If your latest email doesn't get a response, assume the conversation is done, or that your peer is wrecked with stress or workload. Get into the habit of thinking that way: "They must be really busy, hope/glad things are going well for them," rather than this way: "Wow, they didn't even bother to answer me, what a snob."

Because trust the three jaguars: one day you will be that person. So once again:

So all this talk about other artists, but very little talk about meeting them! Let's talk about. . . .

Artists' Organizations

Oh yes! We have them! There are organizations for cartoonists (no painters allowed, and very strict definitions!) to poets and every kind of artist and crafter in between. There are local organizations and national ones. There are tiny ones that offer nothing but a newsgroups now and then, to vast, sprawling ones that even offer group health insurance rates. If you wanted, you could probably spend a huge chunk of money on annual fees for dozens of organizations, and fill your inbox and mailbox with newsletters and glossy member magazines.

The question is . . . do you want to?

Most of us will want to join some form of professional organization. They're a good way to keep abreast of industry news, opportunities and grants, and legal issues that apply to our work. Some organizations offer substantial benefits to members: legal counsel, emergency funds, seminars and classes (naturally in return for substantial fees). But how do you choose? Here are some steps:

1. **Investigate your choices.** Do an internet search for your particular craft and organizations. Go to local shops where your art is sold or taught and check their billboards for local groups. Compile a list of different organizations available to you, their membership requirements, their fees and their benefits. Don't forget to note their locations and where they have their monthly or annual meetings.

2. **Decide on your priorities.** What do you want out of an organization? Are you looking for local meetings so you can hang out with other artists? Do you want more information on grants? Do you need legal help? Do you want to get listed on a specific, highly-trafficked organization's website? Narrow down your choices to the organizations that fulfill the most priorities.

3. **Budget, budget, budget.** Have Business Manager haul out the books and see what kind of money you can allocate to organizational fees. If you only have enough for the one big national organization, is it worth it to you to forgo joining two smaller local or regional groups?

4. **Preview.** If at all possible, try to preview the group. If it's a local one, show up at one of the meetings: most organizations will let you come by for a night to see if it suits you. If it's a larger group, try ordering a copy of their newsletter/magazine, or reading their newsgroup archives to see

if the kind of information they're sharing and the vibe is what you're seeking.

5. **Extended Preview.** Commit to trying out some of these organizations for a year by paying their dues and participating in their events. The only way to really see if you're a good fit for an organization is by trying it out. And if it doesn't suit you, then don't continue paying the dues.

Finally, remember that it's perfectly okay to decide you don't want the hassle of dealing with an artists' organization. There are a lot of benefits to doing so, but if there's nothing out there that works for you, helps you, or introduces you to people you can talk shop with, save your money.

When to Stop Talking

When you get a good chemistry going with a party, a peer, a group, it can be invigorating. Artist is energized by the creative flow and excited by the chance to talk with people who know exactly what she means. It can become very addictive, helping other people with their problems and talking with people more successful than you about their strategies.

So addictive, in fact, that Artist might be tempted to do it all the time. Particularly since Business Manager and Marketer have the lock-down on every other form of communication.

Remember: you're an artist. And getting the work done means you have to stop hanging out, drinking the coffee, and actually paint. Communication is an important business tool, but in the end, the business is without purpose if the Artist doesn't work; Marketer doesn't have anything to sell. Business

Manager doesn't have anything to distribute or license. And eventually, Artist won't have anything to talk to her peers about, having become one of those artists who talks about doing art but never does it.

So put the work first. The communication will take care of itself.

Sample Responses

Positive Situations

- "Oh, sure, I've done crowdfunding before. I've only got a few minutes before my next panel but I can give you a couple of tips. I've also written it up on my website, so you can go there later if you want more information."

- "You know, you're really good at managing people! How did you learn to do that?"

- "So-and-so's really helpful, she's made a lot of money doing things just like this . . . maybe you could ask her about it? She's helped me before."

Negative Situations

- "That artist didn't answer my email about this question I had . . . hm . . . I wonder who else does something similar, that I could ask?"

- "Artist X always makes me feel like a tyro and never seems to say nice things about anyone. I think I'll go see what Artist Y is like, maybe they'll have a more positive attitude."

- "Someone told me that Artist Z said I was a hack. I guess everyone's got an opinion. I'll just get back to work."

Don't Do or Say This:

- "You're so good you make me sick!"

Who wants to hear this? Seriously. It takes a compliment ("you're so good") and forces the person to feel guilt about it ("you make me feel bad"). If you want to compliment another artist, do it without emotional arm-twisting. They're not responsible for your feelings of envy, and forcing it on them is ugly.

In Conclusion

Succeeding as a businessperson inevitably involves relationships. Your goal is to nurture the good ones, and as with all relationships (social or professional), doing so requires good communication. There's a lot to think about in this chapter, and inevitably you're not going to get it all straight or right at first . . . that's okay! Just be mindful about the things you say and write; be polite, kind and keep your priorities straight; and you'll get the hang of it. You'll definitely have plenty of practice!

This concludes our communication topic! We hope our break-down of the different relationships you'll be managing has helped you get a sense for how to more successfully communicate with people on a professional level.

Business for the Right-Brained

Brand

WE'VE SAVED THE BEST chapter for last, the chapter that sums up so many of the concepts we've been discussing for pages and pages. It's about the one thing that reflects everything about you as both an artist and a businessperson, your practices, your style, your products, even how good you are at communication, time management, and other business processes.

That thing is your brand.

And your brand, O Artist, is you.

But wait! You say. Isn't branding a corporate thing? The sort of thing you trademark? I thought only products could be brands . . .

And all that used to be true . . . in the industrial age, maybe. But we've left that century behind, and the one after it . . . and we're well into an age transformed by the internet and a global culture accelerated by social media and interconnectivity. Which is just a fancy way of saying that these days, people don't buy things. They buy experiences. They buy people. They make purchasing decisions on more than whether the product is available and does the job . . . not when they could walk into a store and find sixty versions of the same product, all made by different people and doing slightly different things.

It's a world where if you want to make cookies, you can

choose between twenty different kinds of spatulas . . . or get a personal chef . . . or go to a restaurant . . . or order from a restaurant online and get it delivered to your doorstep within a few hours! And in a world of that many choices, not only between products but also between services, brand is a lot less about a thing and a lot more about who's selling it, how it's sold, and how it makes someone feel to choose it.

Your primary product, then, from this perspective . . . is yourself. You are the thing you're selling to other people. You're taking your thoughts, your heart, and your skills, distributing them into products, and pitching them to a public oversaturated with amazing work. When they buy from you, then, they're not just buying a mug with your art on it or a book with your name on it or a skirt with your tag . . . they're buying into *you*: your career, your vision, and your Grand Plans.

So how do your fans and customers and patrons figure out what your brand is like? And how do you get them to want to support and recommend it? What does it take to make a successful brand?

The Ingredients of a Successful Brand

As the three jaguars see it, here's what you need.

Name

This one seems simple on the face of it, and it is . . . once you figure it out. But once you choose your name, you have to stick with it. If you want to be known as Pink Parasol Designs, then that's the name you're going to be pushing; your business cards, website, social media presences, business license, etc, all should reflect that. So be sure that's what you want, or you may end up saddled with a name you don't want, or doing the laborious and painful work of redirecting an existing audience from a name you've outgrown to one that suits you better.

Personality

The second part of your brand is what your fans, customers, and patrons will perceive as your personality. This is made up equal parts of how you act in public, how you act when dealing with them one-on-one, and the social media presences you project. More and more, personality is making decisions for consumers, not just with small businesses, but with big ones: there are enough choices in the marketplace that people will often reject a business that behaves unethically or rudely in favor of someone just waiting to take their place in the market.

As an artist, your personality is particularly important to people, because it's part of what informs your art, and thus it leaks out into everything you do and all the products you issue. You will have noticed that throughout this book the three jaguars have been talking again and again about positive language, proper behavior in public, and how to deal with negative situations productively. We do not suggest that you try to be someone else; if you're an energetic and vivacious person, don't try to become demure and quiet, or vice versa. But presenting yourself as the best you possible makes a big difference to people trying to decide between buying one artist's work and another.

Genius art will always have buyers, no matter how badly its artists behave. But few of us will have that latitude, and none of us should assume we're going to earn it. Once buyers are done with genius, they often have many different artists whose work entices them, and they're going to make their choices based as much on your brand's ingredients as anything you make. So pay attention to your public presentation. Be courteous, kind, positive, and helpful.

Presence

Closely allied to personality is presence. Our world is becoming habituated to instantaneous response, or at least some way to engage the artist. If a fan buys a CD, they expect a URL on the back taking them to a website where they can learn more. In the flush of their first excitement, they might be hoping for t-shirts . . . or a newsletter they can sign up for, or a social media presence they can follow to keep track of your next album.

If they buy an album and there's nothing in it, no way for them to form a connection or feel like you're a real person they can check on, explore, get to know . . . you will lose them. Fans like to feel a personal connection to the artists they patronize. To the extent that you can be responsive and present online or in personal appearances without cutting into your work time, you should be.

Quality

Just as with a big corporation, the quality of your work is part of your brand. How much time do you dedicate to improving your skills? How much attention to detail is evident in your offerings? How much work do you produce, and is it all up to your standards? Remember that every piece of work you choose to expose to the world is speaking for you, not just as an artist, but as a business.

Quality doesn't just apply to your work either, but to your products. Are they worth the money? Are they well-made? Are they well-designed? Do you back them personally, replacing them if they're broken or subpar? Are you responsive when someone tells you they're not satisfied? If you're producing the products yourself, are you going the extra mile to make sure it's the best thing you can make? If you're distributing your work through someone else, are they meeting your customer's needs (and if not, are you researching alternatives so you can shift your business to them)?

Responsibility

Related to quality, Responsibility is how seriously you take the business portion of your work. The most amazing artist in the world won't get a single sale if she doesn't bother to make the work available, or respond to customers who want it and can't get it, or who've gotten it and think the quality was rotten. Likewise, your fans are watching you to see how often you're producing your work, and forming impressions from that about how hard you work. They do it because they want your next piece, but that data goes into the pot along with thoughts about whether you're really serious about your work. If your fans perceive that you are less serious about your art than they are . . . well.

Time

Finally, the biggest builder of brand . . . is time. You can be the most personable, responsible, noticeable, memorable and skilled artist, and if you are you'll probably make a big splash . . . but unless you put the time in, day after day, you're going to become one of those artists people talk about by saying, "Hey whatever happened to x, she had so much promise."

Time creates audience. Time creates inventory. Time creates buzz. You might have heard people saying 'It took me ten years to become an overnight success.' Don't expect overnight results. Most artists give it a go for a few months, even a year, and are discouraged when they don't have the following or income of an artist who's been at work for two decades. You can't expect results without the secret ten year effort.

And note: the clock doesn't start when you produce one drawing and write a blog or two. Those years of preparation of messing around, trying new things, making half-hearted efforts are just that. Preparation. The day you sit down and begin a sustained effort at art as your Real Job (whether it's paying you or not), the day you get your business license because you've committed yourself to the course . . . that's the start of the years that will lead you to success.

But . . . I Want to Give Up

You've read this book. You've gotten to this point. Maybe the thought of having to put in so much work to make it happen exhausts you. Maybe you're trying it and you aren't enjoying it . . . or maybe you're into year five and it doesn't look like there's any way you're going to make it.

Remember: being an artist, creating work that fulfills you—even a lot of it!—doesn't require you to make a job out of your vocation. You can give up the "business" part without abandoning your creativity. You can certainly be bad at the business part without being awful at the art part; they're not the same thing. (You can also fall in love with the business part, and that doesn't make you any less of an artist!) No matter what happens, the art is the part you should never give up. Whether you make money or not. Whether you have to take a Day Job or not. Whether people love your work or are indifferent or don't even seem to know who you are. Keep going. This gift inside of you is yours, and no one will ever take it away from you.

The jaguars hope you never give up . . . and that if you decide art as a career is for you, that this book has given you some tools to succeed. But remember, whether you go into business or not, the art is forever.

Other Three Jaguars Titles!

BUT WAIT! YOU'RE DONE with this book but you want more? We've got you covered! Check out these Three Jaguars titles:

The Three Jaguars Comic Collection

Being in business as a creative of any type—writer, artist, musician, craftsperson—can be intimidating. The Three Jaguars web comic tackled basic business issues for artists with humor, panache, and fur! Using the archetypes of Artist, Marketer, and Business Manager, the

jaguars took on everything from troubling contract clauses to calculating return on investment. This collection includes the entirety of the 6 month run of the comic, plus bonus material drawn for this volume specifically.

Hugo Award-winning artist Ursula Vernon says "It's better than burning your house down and taking to the sea!" So pull up a chair, a cup of coffee, and join the jaguars for fun, education, and the occasional cuddle picture! (Marketer insisted on that part!)

The Three Jaguars Present: From Spark to Finish: Running Your Kickstarter Campaign

In my first year on Kickstarter, I ran four campaigns. All four succeeded; in fact, all four overfunded, some by over 400%.

I am not a media superstar. I am, at best, a very energetic indie author and freelance painter. But even a small fish can make a big splash in the Kickstarter pond . . . with the right tools. This guide outlines the steps I took to build and fund all of my campaigns, from the spark of an idea, through project design and running the campaign, all the way to fulfillment . . . and beyond. It's even got checklists . . . and of course, cartoon jaguars!

Are you ready to run your own successful Kickstarter campaign? Let's get started!

Business for the Right-Brained

Acknowledgments

THE CHAPTERS IN THIS BOOK first appeared as columns on my Livejournal, crowdfunded before that was even a thing: readers would tip me for them, so I kept writing them. My first thank-you, then, is to all those readers who demonstrated that when you create something of value, people will find a way to compensate you . . . particularly if you ask for their help devising the means. So many people tell me that no one on the internet will pay for things they get for free. The fact that my audience disproves that, over and over, is one of the lasting delights of my tenure online. Thank you all, aletsen.

Likewise, to all the folks who attended my various business seminars at conventions—who in fact, pack the rooms to hear me speak so that there's sometimes only standing room left— thank you so much for coming, listening, and sharing your stories. I've learned as much from you as you have from me.

In the matter of compiling this book, some specifics: to the members of the JaguarHolt Discord server, who tested the various revisions of this book and reported back to me on the behavior of the graphics on their various devices . . . thank you so much. I can't even. I'd say "I'm never doing a graphics-heavy ebook again," but you all know better, and so do I. This is my whimpery face.

To Phil, particularly, for ripping at the guts of the e-book stylesheet to make it work on as many devices as we could figure out . . . this book wouldn't have happened without you. Its readers should send you all the chocolate. I should too, except Petrov will probably get to it first.

Likewise, many thanks go to stalwart designer Dave Bryant, who did a fantastic job with the finicky work of laying out the print edition of the book. Dave is unendingly patient, meticulous, and professional and I'm grateful to have him on my team. (And if you need your own book designer, I highly recommend him: look up Catspaw DTP.)

Lastly, for May, who knows why. This book is dedicated to yuuuuu! Because bestest ever. *purrs*

Business for the Right-Brained

About the Author

I'S TRADITIONAL TO WRITE these sections in third person, but it does sound funny. So I won't! I—M.C.A. Hogarth—am an author of over forty titles in the genres of science fiction, fantasy, humor and romance, as well as a painter and obviously a cartoonist . . . but I've had my foot in the business world all my life, and translating between the business and creative worlds has been one of my enduring interests. I've done lots of other jobs, both outside my chosen profession of art and writing, and within it (like Vice President of SFWA), and all of it is grist for the mill.

You can check out my books on my website, where you can also subscribe to my mailing list, check out my latest Kickstarter, or poke at my Patreon. As always, I'd love to hear from you! Write a comment or a tweet or drop me a line. Tell me about your projects. We're all in this together: let's fill the world with amazing art.

mcahogarth.org
mcahogarth@twitter.com
mcahogarth@patreon.com

Made in the USA
Columbia, SC
19 March 2022